THE COMPOSITION AND NUTRIENT CONTENT OF

FOODS COMMONLY CONSUMED BY

SOUTH ASIANS IN THE UK

Patricia A Judd, Tashmin Kassam-Khamis, Jane E Thomas

Department of Nutrition and Dietetics

King's College London, UK

The Aga Khan Health Board for the United Kingdom

i

ISBN 0-9537882-3-7

Front Cover photographs courtesy of Tommy Miah
Printed by Keyprint, Edinburgh

CONTENTS

Aga Khan Health Board for the United Kingdom

The Aga Khan Health Board for the United Kingdom is made up entirely of volunteers with a mandate to devise and implement strategies for improving health services and standards of health. It works with the Aga Khan Health Services, which is a not-for-profit international network of institutions operating in Asia and Africa helping people of all religious and ethnic identities by:

1. Establishing, promoting and undertaking health awareness initiatives.

2. Conceptualising, establishing, organising, supporting and operating programmes promoting primary health care and other projects for the prevention, treatment, and elimination of diseases and sickness of all kinds.

3. Working with other institutions and programmes having similar aims and objectives.

In the United Kingdom, The Aga Khan Health Board is committed to improving access to health services and information on healthy lifestyles within the context of the established health and cultural practices of the different South Asian groups. These aims are achieved through a variety of health promotional activities, "Health and Fitness" road shows, "First-Aid" training programmes and "Special Needs" fora. The Board has developed mechanisms for identifying gaps in health information by monitoring health and disease trends, within the Ismaili community.

Where areas for action have been highlighted, the Board has undertaken research that contributes to the understanding of the specific needs of the diverse South Asian communities in Britain. This publication is the direct result of collaboration between the Aga Khan Health Board (UK), The Department of Health, King's College, London and The Aga Khan Foundation (UK) to produce data with academic rigour to contribute to the National sources of public health information. The Board would like to acknowledge the tremendous support received from numerous individuals in preparing the data for this publication. We are eternally grateful to Patricia Judd, Azmina Govindji and Jane Thomas for their steadfast and unrelenting support.

We hope this publication will prove of value to all those with an interest in effective health promotion.

Mahmood Poonja
Chairman
December 1999

The Ismaili Centre, 1 Cromwell Gardens, London SW7 2SL
Telephone: 020 7581 2071 Fax: 020 7589 3246

FOREWORD

Since the 1980's research has increasingly shown that people of South Asian origin in Britain have higher rates of cardiovascular disease and diabetes. Advice about diet and lifestyle plays a vital role in the prevention and management of these conditions as well as other health promotion activities. In order for advice to be effective it must be tailored to be culturally appropriate. This involves recognition of the diversity of the South Asian population. In Britain, there are some 3 million people of South Asian origin. Their families have come from countries across the sub-continent and include diverse religious groupings from India, Gujarat, (Hindus/Jains) and the Punjab (Sikhs); from Pakistan (Muslims); from Bangladesh (Muslims); and via East Africa (Hindus and Muslims).

The stimulus for the work on which this publication is based was an observation in the late 1980s by Dr Azim Lakhani, then Chair of the Aga Khan Health Board (AKHB) for the UK. He and the members of the AHKB noted that provision of dietary advice for people originating from South Asia (India, Pakistan and Bangladesh) was hampered by the lack of information on the composition of the foods most commonly eaten by the different groups. In 1990, as a member of the AKHB and Chief Dietician to the British Diabetic Association (DDA), I conducted a survey amongst dietitians working in regions of high South Asian population in the UK. The findings confirmed overwhelmingly that there was a need for this type of data to cater for the health promotion needs of the growing ethnic minority population.
Joint funding from the Aga Khan Foundation (UK) and the Department of Health enabled a project to be set up to determine the foods most commonly consumed by the different South Asian groups and ascertain the nutrient content both by calculation and in some cases by direct laboratory analysis. Further funding from the Ministry of Agriculture, Fisheries and Food (MAFF), allowed the project to be extended to obtain further information about eating patterns that might aid provision of health education strategies for these groups.

In 1992, the Government of the day published a strategy paper *'The Health of the Nation'*, for England and Wales, which highlighted coronary heart disease and stroke as key areas for prevention. The Government declared support for a variety of projects aimed at the specific needs of black and ethnic minority groups, including funding and support granted by the Department of Health to the Aga Khan Foundation (UK) to undertake this study entitled - *'An Analysis of Asian foods to help formulate accurate and relevant advice to the Asian population on diet.'*

The 1999 Government White Paper *' Saving Lives - Our Healthier Nation'* also highlights the need for targeting ethnic minority groups. The Paper recognises that death rates for coronary heart disease within the South Asian communities are 38% higher for men and 43% higher for women than in the wider population. The strategy for targeting prevention, care and treatment is particularly relevant to people from black and ethnic minority groups.

People are in a better position to take care of their health if they have the opportunity to make informed decisions. Until now, specific information on the nutritional composition of the diverse range of South Asian cooked foods has not been available. State Registered Dietitians and other healthcare professionals, equipped with this data, will now be able to deliver dietary advice and health promotion better tailored to individual habits and promote targeted health education and treatment. This data will help in the management of existing heart disease and diabetes. It will also provide an informed basis for the development of prevention strategies, which may be used in the context of healthy living centres, supporting people within a local community setting. The cooked dishes within this book have been categorised according to the ingredients and cooking methods adopted by the South Asian groups, hence making it easy for users to access information appropriate to individual needs. For example, the Punjabi dishes are more likely to be representative of the predominantly Sikh population in Southall, whereas the Gujarati data will be particularly appropriate to the Hindu communities in Leicester.

A significant finding of this project is the variation, both between and within communities, of the ingredients as well as cooking methods of dishes with similar names. The results of this study, concerning both food composition and eating habits, show the potential value of such hard work in the context of national strategies for health. Valuable as this data is, however, more work remains to be done, including an expansion of the range of foods for which compositional data is available.

The AKHB is also committed to the dissemination of the findings of this research. Health education strategies are planned, subject to funding, for the data to be disseminated to the relevant South Asian groups by means of healthy living centres, broadcast media and the Asian press.

In conclusion, the results of this study, conducted as part of a PhD programme at King's College London, represent an important partnership where members of the community, academic institutions and the Government work together to improve health.

Azmina Govindji BSc SRD
State Registered Dietitian
Project Co-ordinator for AKHB, UK

4

ACKNOWLEDGEMENTS

The work on which this publication is based was initiated by Dr Azim Lakhani, formerly Chair, and other members of the Aga Khan Health Board (AKHB) for the UK. Particular recognition must be given to the work of Mrs. Azmina Govindji who has been instrumental at every stage of this project; from the preliminary study to establish the need for research in this area, through active participation as a member of the AKHB and the steering group to the publication of this book.

Funding for the project was received from the Aga Khan Foundation (AKF, UK), the Department of Health and The Ministry of Agriculture Fisheries and Food (MAFF).

The original steering group for the project consisted of representatives from all interested bodies in addition to the authors:

Mrs Naznin Coker (AKHB), Dr Shahenaz Walji (AKHB), Mrs Azmina Govindji (AKHB), Mrs Veena Bahl (Department of Health), Dr Azim Lakhani (AKF, UK), Mirza Jehani (AKF, UK). Adele Woods (AKF, UK), Dr Paul McKeigue (London School of Hygiene and Tropical Medicine, LSHTM), and Dr El-Nasir Lalani (AKHB). As membership of the AKHB and AKF changed, other parties joined the Steering Group, both formally and informally, to whom the authors owe a debt of gratitude.

The authors are also indebted to the following, without whose assistance the data could not have been collected, analysed or processed: Ms Leena Sevak (LSHTM), Mrs Smita Ganatra and Dr Sheela Reddy for allowing access to the diet records from their various dietary surveys; Mrs Shaheen Sheikh and Mrs Taslima Rana, who acted as link workers and translators for the Pakistani and Bengali groups; Mrs Majda Butt for rechecking the Punjabi recipes; Dr Hans Englyst (Dunn Nutrition Laboratories, Cambridge), Dr Sanoja Sanduradura, Dr Elizabeth Bowey, Mrs Rosie Calokotsia and Miss Emma West for various aspects of the laboratory analysis; Mrs Georgina West (BDA) and Salima Hirani (AKHB) for administrative support.

Last, but by no means least, we wish to thank the people who provided us with the data, answering our questions with patience and allowing us to watch, weigh and measure while they cooked in order to obtain accurate estimates for their recipes.

Patricia A Judd, Tashmin Kassam-Khamis, Jane E Thomas

INTRODUCTION

Gathering information about the nutrient intakes of individuals and groups is notoriously difficult because of the huge variety of foods and products now available and the difficulties of estimating accurately what is eaten on a day to day basis. In the UK this has been facilitated for many years by the food composition tables first published in 1940 by McCance and Widdowson and now into the 5the Edition (Holland et al. 1991). The food tables have increasingly made available values for the nutrient composition of foods eaten by minority groups in the UK, specifically in the Immigrant Foods Supplement (Tan, Wenlock, and Buss, 1985). Nonetheless, in the light of growing concern about the high rates of cardiovascular disease and diabetes mellitus among people of South Asian origin in Britain attention has increasingly focused on the need for more information about the composition of South Asian foods and diets. Without this data it is extremely difficult to fully understand the aetiology of such conditions or to improve dietary management.

Within the South Asian communities in the UK there are people who originate from different parts of the Indian sub-continent and in addition there are dietary differences according to culture and religion which result in a variety of traditional diets. Added to these inherent differences in food habits are the effects which migration may have on the choice of individual dishes (possibly due to availability of ingredients) and the way they are prepared. These differences often go unrecognised and have resulted in a perception of an "Asian" diet which may not accurately reflect that of any individual group.

The data collected in this book is the culmination of a project which set out to identify the traditional dishes most commonly eaten by the different South Asian groups in the UK and to collect recipes for these from the people preparing them. For the purposes of data collection the groups were divided as follows:

Sikhs originating mainly in the Punjab, Hindus from Gujarat, and three Muslim groups ; Pakistanis, Bengalis and Ismailis (mostly originating from Gujarat but coming to the UK via East Africa). Information is therefore provided here which identifies the dishes most commonly eaten by each group, together with recipes for each dish and the corresponding nutrient composition. We hope that dietitians and others working with members of South Asian communities will find the information helpful.

DATA COLLECTION AND ANALYSIS

The information concerning the composition of foods presented in this report arose from two distinct sources.

Firstly, a number of studies have been undertaken among South Asian populations in the UK to investigate aspects of the aetiology of degenerative diseases which have included measures of dietary intake. Access to this data provided the opportunity to examine the dishes commonly consumed and, since details of recipes had also been collected, the ability to calculate the nutrient composition of the dishes. Secondly, for some South Asian groups where little data was available it was necessary to initiate the essential data collection.

Gujarati and Punjabi Data

At the outset of the project it became apparent that recipe data had been collected in various projects investigating dietary intakes within the communities originating in Gujarat and the Punjab. Access was given to the 7 day diet records obtained from 88 Punjabi Sikh men in Southall (Sevak et al. 1994) and the Gujarati data was collected from two surveys in West London; Reddy (1991) obtained 7 day weighed records from 23 vegetarian females, mainly from Harrow in West London and Ganatra (personal communication) five day records from 20 men living in Wembley. In all three studies recipe data was available in the form of weighed ingredients plus the cooked weight of the recipe which enabled calculation of nutrient content per 100g food.

The Punjabi records yielded 379 recipes for 87 different dishes and the Gujarati data 67 recipes for 40 dishes. The nutrient content of all dishes for which more than one recipe existed was calculated and data has been presented elsewhere showing the variability of the recipes and nutrient composition (Kassam - Khamis et al. 1995).

Bangladeshi, Ismaili and Pakistani Data

As there was little data available for these three groups a study was initiated to ascertain the dishes most commonly consumed by each group and to obtain representative recipes from them. Thirty households in each group (291 individuals aged over 12 years) were asked to keep dietary records for 7 days which detailed all foods eaten. Once the most common traditional dishes had been identified, three recipes for each dish were obtained by going back to households where the food had been eaten during the survey. The main cook was asked to weigh all ingredients as well as the final cooked weight of the dish next time it was prepared. For some Pakistani and Bangladeshi households, where literacy was a problem, one of the authors (TKK), together with a translator, was present to weigh and record the ingredients and final cooked weight of the dish.

Selection of recipes

The recipes chosen for presentation here are those which had been eaten by at least 20% of the participants during the 5 or 7 day survey periods (See Appendix 1a). In each case the nutrient content of the recipe with the energy and fat content nearest the mean for all values for that dish is presented. If only two recipes were available for a dish, that with the highest energy and fat content is presented.

The ingredients for each recipe together with cooked weights and method of preparation are given in the 'Recipe' section starting on page 68. In addition, the ingredients list for the lowest energy and fat version of each dish, together with the energy and proximate nutrient content, are presented alongside.

Calculation of nutrient content

The nutrient content of the cooked recipes was calculated using the Comp-eat dietary analysis program (Version 4.0, Lifeline UK) which uses data from the 5the edition of The Composition of Foods (Holland et al. 1991) and the available supplements, including the Cereals Supplement (Holland et al. 1988) and the most recent values for vegetables, herbs and spices (Holland et al. 1991a). Values were added to the data base using available analytical data for certain foods, for example the fish imported from Bangladesh. The ingredients, with the weight of each used was entered into the analysis programme together with the estimate of water lost, derived from the final cooked weight of the dish. This enabled calculation of the nutrient content per 100g of cooked food. As raw ingredients were used in the calculations, vitamin contents were adjusted to allow for cooking losses as described in The Composition of Foods 1991 and detailed in Appendix 2.

For certain foods, values for particular nutrients were not available for some ingredients. Problems arose mainly for pulses, the Bangladeshi fish and certain spices. Appendix 3 outlines the range of missing values. Where possible the nutrient value for a similar food was substituted and an estimate made of the nutrient content of the recipe. With respect to the spices, such adjustments were only made if the ingredients made up more than 3% of the final cooked weight of a dish. In some cases no appropriate substitute value could be found and in these cases it has been indicated that the dish may be a useful source of the nutrient but that no estimate of nutrient amount can be given.

Laboratory analysis

For selected items, laboratory analysis of a range of nutrients was carried out as follows:

a. Purchased dishes.

Samples of traditional foods, commonly consumed but not usually made at home, were purchased in retail outlets used by the subjects (3 samples of each food) and subjected to laboratory analysis.

b. Bangladeshi fish.

Samples of fish commonly used by the Bangladeshi participants (see Appendix 1b) were obtained from retail outlets in East London and analysed in duplicate. These values were then entered into the data base for calculation of the nutrient content of dishes containing them.

Analytical values are available for energy and a range of nutrients as follows:

Protein, carbohydrate, fat, sodium, potassium, calcium, iron, zinc (for all the above), fatty acids, folate and vitamin C (for purchased dishes only).

Details of the methods used for analysis are given on page 15 with the Food Composition Tables.

USES AND ABUSES OF THE TABLES

As with any food composition data, the nutrient composition data given here cannot be regarded as absolute. We have attempted to give an estimate of the nutrient composition of a representative sample of each of the dishes we found to be consumed most commonly by the subjects studied in the different South Asian populations, as prepared and cooked by the participants. In the main tables the most important ingredients in each dish have been listed in descending order by weight to facilitate an appropriate choice of recipe. However, as has been demonstrated elsewhere (Kassam - Khamis et al. 1995), there is considerable variation in the nutrient content of the dishes when cooked by different individuals and as with any "made-up dish", whether it be Shepherds pie or aubergine and tomato bhaji, probably varies from day to day when cooked by the same individual. These factors should be kept in mind when using the data in dietary surveys or for determination of individual intakes.

For some particular nutrients such as fatty acids and the water-soluble vitamins, special care may be necessary. The fatty acid content given in the main table (and in the tables expressing the values from laboratory analysis) was derived using the fats and oils described in the recipes, whether butter ghee, vegetable ghee, mixed vegetable oil, corn oil or others - as outlined in the second column of the main table. In order to obtain appropriate values for individuals it would be necessary to ascertain the specific type of fat used in cooking. With respect to water-soluble vitamins, the values for raw foods have been adjusted to allow for cooking losses as described in the 5the edition of The Composition of Foods, 1991 and outlined in Appendix 4. These values can only be approximate as the cooking times for some of the dishes described here may be much longer than the times used to cook vegetables alone.

The recipe data extracted from the surveys of the Punjabi and Gujarati participants did not include the amounts of salt or spices used in the dishes. In the recipes the use of salt and the most common types of spices are indicated in parentheses but no amounts have been added into the calculations. This means that the sodium and chloride content is underestimated as well as the content of other nutrients such as potassium, iron and trace elements.

The findings, interpretations and conclusions expressed in this paper are entirely those of the authors and do not necessarily state or reflect those of the Aga Khan Foundation (UK).

Uses in health education

Although diet is only one factor in the aetiology of heart disease and diabetes it is an important determinant, together with exercise, in controlling body weight and possibly influences other risk factors for disease. The recipes we have chosen to give for each dish are those where the energy and fat content was nearest the mean for the several recipes collected for each dish. This implies that some people were preparing dishes with energy and fat content higher than those presented here and that others made similar dishes which were much lower in energy and fat.

In terms of health education it may be desirable to suggest reduction in energy and fat in the diets of many individuals and therefore when alternative lower fat versions were available for a dish we have listed the ingredients and calculated values for energy and proximate nutrients (protein, fat and carbohydrate) for the recipe which is lowest in energy and fat content. This recipe was in each case supplied by a participant whose family presumably found it acceptable and satisfying and might therefore be used as an example of a traditional dish cooked in a 'healthier' way.

Close inspection of the recipes demonstrates that there are several possible ways in which the lower fat version may differ from the average version. In some dishes especially, but not exclusively, vegetable dishes it is sometimes simply that less fat or oil is used for similar amounts of other ingredients. In dishes where meat provides a high proportion of the fat, the lower fat version often has a higher proportion of other ingredients such as vegetables than the higher energy and fat versions, thus diluting the effect of the meat. Each of these strategies can be suggested to individuals or groups as methods of modifying their own recipes, even when the absolute nutrient content is not known.

In some recipes it will be noted that the differences in nutrient content are due to the higher water content. This is noticeable with the dhals - a thin dhal will often be lower in fat and other nutrients than a thick dhal and care is necessary here. It may be that a larger portion of the thinner dhals is eaten than the thicker dhals, cancelling out the beneficial effects. This book does not attempt to give portion sizes for the foods eaten by the different South Asian groups.

In addition, knowledge of the amount and types of fats or oils commonly used by individuals and groups may enable health workers to target specific dishes. Practical advice can be given, for example, measuring the fat in dhals/curries rather than simply pouring an unknown amount into the pan.

ARRANGEMENT OF THE TABLES

In the Main Food Composition Tables (Section 1) the data has been arranged by groups of types of recipe ie vegetable dishes, pulse dishes, rice-based dishes, breads, meat dishes, fish dishes and sweet dishes. Within each overall group there are dishes with similar names and ingredients cooked by the different groups of people. For example there are recipes for 'chicken curry' obtained from the Punjabi, Pakistani, Ismaili and Bengali participants.

Section 2 of the Food Composition Tables gives the energy value and the values for a range of nutrients for the foods which were purchased and analysed in the laboratory. This includes the imported Bengali fish and some dishes which were purchased in retail outlets.

In the Recipe section, the ingredients, weight of ingredients and final cooked weight of the dish is given for the recipe for which the nutrient content is provided in Section 1 of the main table, together with a brief outline of the cooking method. Alongside this is given the weight of ingredients, final cooked weight and the water, energy and proximate nutrient content of the corresponding recipe which had the lowest energy and fat content. The recipes are arranged in the same order as in the main table.

SYMBOLS AND ABBREVIATIONS USED IN THE TABLES

Symbols

0	None of the nutrient is present
Tr	Trace
Bold type	Estimated value
N	Significant amount present but no value available

Abbreviations

CHO	carbohydrate
NSP	non-starch polysaccharides (Englyst Method)
MUFA	monounsaturated fatty acids
PUFA	polyunsaturated fatty acids
SFA	saturated fatty acids
REQ	retinol equivalents
Sunfl.	sunflower
Saffl.	safflower
Veg.	vegetable
Chol	cholesterol
Tom.	tomato

THE FOOD COMPOSITION TABLES

Section 1

Calculated energy and nutrient content of commonly consumed traditional foods.

Section 2

Analytical values for commonly consumed purchased dishes and Bangladeshi fish.

ANALYTICAL METHODS USED FOR NUTRIENTS IN SECTION 2

Constituent	Method
Water	Air oven at 100° C or Vacuum freeze drying
Nitrogen	Kjeldhal procedure
Fat	Soxhlet method
Fatty Acids	GLC of methyl esters (IUPAC 1976)
Total Carbohydrate	By difference
Non-Starch Polysaccharides	Englyst and Cummings (1984, 1988)
Sodium and Potassium	Flame photometry
Calcium, iron and zinc	Atomic absorption spectrometry
Ascorbic Acid	Titrimetry (AOAC 1975)
Folate	Microbiological assay (Philips and Wright 1983, Bell 1974)

SECTION 1

Composition of food per 100g

Vegetable dishes 1 - 16

No	Recipe	Main Ingredients	Water g	Protein g	Fat g	CHO g	Energy kcals	Energy kj
1	Punjabi mixed veg. curry	carrots, peas, potatoes, corn oil	74.0	2.5	9.8	11.2	140	581
2	Gujarati mixed veg. curry	peas, aubergine, tomatoes, corn oil	81.8	3.6	4.4	6.3	78	325
3	Ismaili mixed veg. curry	new pots, frozen mix veg, onions, tomato, sunfl. oil	78.9	2.2	4.2	11.4	89	374
4	Pakistani mixed veg. curry	frozen mixed veg, onions, tomatoes, sunfl. oil	83.7	2.8	1.5	7.5	51	217
5	Bengali mixed veg. bhaji	frozen mix veg, onions, new pots, veg. oil, tomatoes	63.5	2.5	19.7	11.2	229	947
6	Punjabi spinach curry	spinach, onions, cornflour, butter ghee	85.5	2.4	2.4	5.7	53	220
7	Gujarati spinach curry	spinach, tomatoes, veg. oil	73.9	2.9	14.2	3.0	151	622
8	Pakistani spinach curry (palak)	spinach, butter ghee, onions, chilli, chick pea flour	78.2	3.0	9.2	3.7	109	450
9	Bengali spinach bhaji	spinach, onions, sunfl. oil, coriander	60.2	6.8	10.8	5.1	145	596
10	Gujarati methi bhaji	spinach, veg oil, fenugreek seeds	72.5	5.8	6.5	7.8	111	460
11	Punjabi spinach/potato	spinach, old pots, sunfl. oil	72.9	3.5	8.3	10.1	127	529
12	Punjabi aubergine bhaji	aubergines, onions, tomatoes, vegetable oil	71.2	2.4	8.1	14.2	135	564
13	Gujarati aubergine bhaji	aubergine, corn oil	85.9	0.8	7.7	2.0	80	330
14	Gujarati aubergine curry	aubergine, tomatoes, peanut oil	81.4	0.9	12.2	2.4	122	503
15	Punjabi aubergine/potato curry	aubergine, onions, old pots, tomatoes, corn oil	80.8	1.5	6.7	8.3	96	399
16	Gujarati potato curry	old potatoes, corn oil	71.7	2.3	5.9	18.5	132	554

Vegetable dishes 1 - 16

Composition of food per 100g

No	Recipe	PUFA g	MUFA g	SFA g	Chol mg	Starch g	Sugar g	NSP g
1	Punjabi mixed veg.curry	5.7	2.4	1.3	0	5.6	4.5	2.6
2	Gujarati mixed veg. curry	2.5	1.0	0.6	0	2.7	2.2	3.5
3	Ismaili mixed veg. curry	2.5	0.8	0.5	0	8.0	3.1	1.6
4	Pakistani mixed veg. curry	0.6	0.2	0.1	0	2.2	4.3	2.5
5	Bengali mixed veg. bhaji	9.4	6.8	2.0	0	6.4	3.9	3.0
6	Punjabi spinach curry	0.5	0.5	1.2	5	4.1	1.5	1.8
7	Gujarati spinach curry	7.0	4.9	1.5	0	0.1	2.9	2.4
8	Pakistani spinach curry (palak)	0.8	2.1	5.6	23	1.6	1.8	2.2
9	Bengali spinach bhaji	6.8	2.0	1.3	0	0.8	4.1	4.9
10	Gujarati methi bhaji	3.7	3.1	0.8	0	0.2	3.1	3.5
11	Punjabi spinach/potato	5.2	1.6	1.0	0	8.5	1.6	2.5
12	Punjabi aubergine bhaji	3.9	2.7	0.9	0	7.5	5.3	2.7
13	Gujarati aubergine bhaji	4.4	1.8	1.0	0	0.2	1.8	1.8
14	Gujarati aubergine curry	3.5	5.7	2.3	0	0.2	2.2	1.6
15	Punjabi aubergine/potato curry	3.8	1.6	0.8	0	4.4	3.2	1.7
16	Gujarati potato curry	3.4	1.4	0.7	0	17.9	0.7	1.4

Vegetable dishes 1 - 16

Inorganic constituents per 100g

No	Recipe	Na mg	K mg	Ca mg	Mg mg	P mg	Fe mg	Cu mg	Zn mg	Cl mg
1	Punjabi mixed veg. curry	15	257	23	14	45	0.7	0.05	0.4	48
2	Gujarati mixed veg. curry	3	178	22	18	59	1.0	0.02	0.6	21
3	Ismaili mixed veg. curry	513	284	22	19	43	0.6	0.08	0.3	818
4	Pakistani mixed veg. curry	428	176	36	17	53	0.9	0.04	0.4	662
5	Bengali mixed veg. bhaji	281	227	27	15	49	0.6	0.06	0.3	451
6	Punjabi spinach curry	117	415	137	44	40	1.8	0.04	0.6	88
7	Gujarati spinach curry	131	575	157	52	53	2.1	0.04	0.7	116
8	Pakistani spinach curry (palak)	562	457	146	52	50	2.0	0.06	0.7	774
9	Bengali spinach bhaji	2203	1173	383	136	114	4.9	0.11	1.6	3142
10	Gujarati methi bhaji	183	733	226	83	90	4.6	0.22	1.5	140
11	Punjabi spinach/potato	121	597	142	53	59	2.0	0.07	0.7	119
12	Punjabi aubergine bhaji	17	425	25	19	48	0.6	0.09	0.4	75
13	Gujarati aubergine bhaji	2	200	10	11	15	0.4	0.01	0.2	13
14	Gujarati aubergine curry	12	221	11	11	17	0.3	0.03	0.2	36
15	Punjabi aubergine/potato curry	13	270	16	12	29	0.4	0.05	0.2	51
16	Gujarati potato curry	8	388	5	18	40	0.4	0.09	0.3	71

Vegetable dishes 1 - 16

Vitamin content per 100g

No	Recipe	REQ ug	Vit. D ug	Vit. E mg	Vit. B1 mg	Vit. B2 mg	Niacin mg	Vit. B6 mg	Vit. B12 ug	Folate ug	Vit. C mg
1	Punjabi mixed veg. curry	387	0	2.05	0.15	0.02	1.1	0.19	0	18	6
2	Gujarati mixed veg. curry	54	0	0.9	0.16	0.05	1.6	0.07	0	27	6
3	Ismaili mixed veg. curry	127	0	2.28	0.11	0.03	0.9	0.24	0	16	8
4	Pakistani mixed veg. curry	285	0	0.58	0.09	0.05	1.0	0.10	0	18	5
5	Bengali mixed veg. bhaji	185	0	0.13	0.12	0.04	1.0	0.22	0	19	8
6	Punjabi spinach curry	484	Tr	1.44	0.05	0.06	1.3	0.12	0	60	11
7	Gujarati spinach curry	583	0	2.15	0.09	0.07	1.8	0.18	0	72	16
8	Pakistani spinach curry (palak)	548	0.2	1.78	0.06	0.06	1.4	0.14	0	64	11
9	Bengali spinach bhaji	1295	0	8.17	0.14	0.17	3.6	0.34	0	166	33
10	Gujarati methi bhaji	733	0	**3.18**	0.11	0.11	2.5	N	0	97	17
11	Punjabi spinach/potato	483	0	5.16	0.13	0.06	1.7	0.29	0	70	13
12	Punjabi aubergine bhaji	18	0	0.48	0.15	0.02	1.1	0.30	0	19	6
13	Gujarati aubergine bhaji	11	0	1.29	0.02	0.01	0.2	0.06	0	8	2
14	Gujarati aubergine curry	19	0	2.15	0.02	0.01	0.4	0.07	0	8	3
15	Punjabi aubergine/potato curry	24	0	1.41	0.09	0.01	0.7	0.18	0	12	4
16	Gujarati potato curry	0	0	1.05	0.18	0.02	1.0	0.38	0	19	6

19

Vegetable dishes 17 - 33

Composition of food per 100g

No	Recipe	Main Ingredients	Water g	Protein g	Fat g	CHO g	Energy kcals	Energy kj
17	Pakistani potato curry	new pots, tomatoes, onions, corn oil	80.2	1.3	8.5	7.8	109	451
18	Bengali potato bhaji	old pots, onions, green peppers, veg. oil	69.4	2.4	5.7	18.7	130	546
19	Punjabi potato/onion/tomato	old pots, tomatoes, onions, sunfl. oil	86.6	0.8	6.0	5.9	79	328
20	Punjabi potato/green pepper	old pots, green pepper, tomatoes, corn oil, onions	70.9	2.2	9.1	15.5	149	621
21	Gujarati potato/tomato	old pots, tomatoes, veg. oil	79.4	1.2	8.9	9.5	121	503
22	Pakistani aloo pakora	chickpea flour, old pots, sunfl. oil, onion, spinach	35.2	10.3	16.3	28.8	293	1228
23	Punjabi potato/courgette	old pots, courgette, tom. puree, onions, sunfl. oil	75.2	2.5	7.2	11.6	118	492
24	Punjabi bhindi	okra, onions, tomatoes, corn oil	79.1	1.9	10.7	4.2	119	492
25	Gujarati bhindi	okra, veg. oil	53.8	3.3	31.8	3.5	312	1285
26	Gujarati bhindi/tomato	okra, tomatoes, corn oil	84.5	2.2	4.9	3.5	66	273
27	Pakistani bhindi	okra, sunflower oil, onions, tomatoes	81.7	1.7	7.2	4.5	86	357
28	Punjabi courgette	courgette, onions, tomatoes, corn oil, chilli	75.2	3.1	12.0	5.7	141	583
29	Punjabi marrow	marrow, tomatoes, veg. oil	84.2	1.1	7.2	4.5	86	358
30	Punjabi carrots/peas/potato	carrots, peas, potatoes, onions, butter	76.7	2.5	6.1	11.3	105	438
31	Punjabi carrots/peas	carrots, peas, butter ghee	72.4	1.9	13.8	9.1	165	683
32	Punjabi carrots/potato	carrots, potatoes, onions, sunfl. oil	67.5	1.9	12.4	15.6	177	735
33	Punjabi green chilli/carrots	carrot, veg. oil, green chilli	81.9	0.7	7.8	8.0	103	428

Vegetable dishes 17 - 33

Composition of food per 100g

No	Recipe	PUFA g	MUFA g	SFA g	Chol mg	Starch g	Sugar g	NSP g
17	Pakistani potato curry	4.8	2.1	1.1	0	5.8	1.8	0.7
18	Bengali potato bhaji	2.7	1.9	0.6	0	16.7	1.6	1.6
19	Punjabi potato/onion/tomato	3.7	1.2	0.7	0	4.8	0.9	0.6
20	Punjabi potato/green pepper	5.2	2.2	1.1	0	13.7	1.7	1.6
21	Gujarati potato/tomato	4.3	3.1	0.9	0	8.8	0.7	0.8
22	Pakistani alco pakora	9.8	3.3	1.8	0	25.1	1.9	5.6
23	Punjabi potato/courgette	4.5	1.4	0.9	0	8.3	3.1	1.5
24	Punjabi bhindi	6.0	2.6	1.4	0	0.6	3.0	2.4
25	Gujarati bhindi	15.1	11.0	3.5	0	0.6	2.9	4.6
26	Gujarati bhindi/tomato	2.7	1.1	0.7	0	0.4	3.1	2.7
27	Pakistani bhndi	4.3	1.5	0.9	0	0.2	3.5	2.2
28	Punjabi courgette	6.8	2.8	1.6	0	0.7	4.4	1.8
29	Punjabi marrow	3.3	2.4	0.7	0	0.7	3.8	1.0
30	Punjabi carrots/peas/potato	0.5	1.4	3.7	15	4.0	6.4	3.3
31	Punjabi carrots/peas	0.7	3.2	8.9	37	1.4	7.1	3.3
32	Punjabi carrots/potato	7.7	2.4	1.5	0	9.6	5.5	2.4
33	Punjabi green chilli/carrots	3.8	2.7	0.9	0	0.6	7.2	2.4

21

Vegetable dishes 17 - 33

Inorganic constituents per 100g

No	Recipe	Na mg	K mg	Ca mg	Mg mg	P mg	Fe mg	Cu mg	Zn mg	Cl mg
17	Pakistani potato curry	268	226	16	15	27	0.7	0.07	0.2	434
18	Bengali potato bhaji	616	402	11	24	45	0.6	0.10	0.4	1009
19	Punjabi potato/onion/tomato	7	145	5	7	15	0.2	0.04	0.1	32
20	Punjabi potato/green pepper	16	368	9	18	40	0.5	0.08	0.3	78
21	Gujarati potato/tomato	8	220	4	10	22	0.3	0.05	0.2	46
22	Pakistani aloo pakora	347	631	104	71	180	4.5	0.33	1.6	546
23	Punjabi potato/courgette	36	480	21	24	53	0.8	0.12	0.4	117
24	Punjabi bhindi	11	250	84	37	41	0.7	0.09	0.4	42
25	Gujarati bhindi	9	383	186	82	68	1.3	0.15	0.7	48
26	Gujarati bhindi/tomato	27	335	99	47	45	0.9	0.12	0.4	78
27	Pakistani bhindi	273	245	77	35	41	0.8	0.08	0.4	446
28	Punjabi courgette	21	580	42	33	74	1.3	0.06	0.5	101
29	Punjabi marrow	9	271	31	19	34	0.4	0.04	0.4	64
30	Punjabi carrots/peas/potato	80	259	33	14	47	0.9	0.05	0.4	133
31	Punjabi carrots/peas	28	207	31	10	36	0.7	0.03	0.3	45
32	Punjabi carrots/potato	25	349	23	14	39	0.6	0.07	0.3	69
33	Punjabi green chilli/carrots	35	175	25	4	17	0.3	0.02	0.1	50

Vegetable dishes 17 - 33

Vitamin content per 100g

No	Recipe	REQ ug	Vit. D ug	Vit. E mg	Vit. B$_1$ mg	Vit. B$_2$ mg	Niacin mg	Vit. B$_6$ mg	Vit. B$_{12}$ ug	Folate ug	Vit. C mg
17	Pakistani potato curry	10	0	1.7	0.06	0.02	0.5	0.17	0	7	6
18	Bengali potato bhaji	4	0	0.17	0.18	0.02	1.0	0.39	0	20	11
19	Punjabi potato/onion/tomato	5	0	3.08	0.06	0.01	0.4	0.12	0	6	2
20	Punjabi potato/green pepper	17	0	1.92	0.15	0.02	0.9	0.35	0	19	17
21	Gujarati potato/tomato	4	0	0.18	0.10	0.01	0.5	0.20	0	10	4
22	Pakistani aloo pakora	51	0	8.07	0.21	0.1	2.1	0.31	0	50	2
23	Punjabi potato/courgette	147	0	4.10	0.15	0.02	1.1	0.28	0	22	9
24	Punjabi bhindi	47	0	2.02	0.11	0.02	0.9	0.14	0	24	7
25	Gujarati bhindi	99	0	0	0.18	0.06	1.3	0.19	0	51	12
26	Gujarati bhindi/tomato	70	0	N	0.11	0.04	1.0	0.14	0	28	10
27	Pakistani bhindi	54	0	3.54	0.11	0.02	0.9	0.14	0	22	7
28	Punjabi courgette	147	0	2.32	0.16	0.02	1.0	0.22	0	37	16
29	Punjabi marrow	36	0	0.12	0.11	Tr	0.5	0.06	0	11	10
30	Punjabi carrots/peas/potato	1031	0.1	0.6	0.16	0.04	1.1	0.17	0	18	5
31	Punjabi carrots/peas	1313	0.3	0.97	0.13	0.03	0.8	0.12	0	14	5
32	Punjabi carrots/potato	791	0	6.30	0.16	0.02	0.8	0.29	0	14	5
33	Punjabi green chilli/carrots	1277	0	0.55	0.08	0.01	0.3	0.11	0	6	3

Vegetable dishes 34 - 51

Composition of food per 100g

No	Recipe	Main Ingredients	Water g	Protein g	Fat g	CHO g	Energy kcals	Energy kj
34	Punjabi cabbage	cabbage, onions, ginger, soya oil	85.6	1.8	3.1	6.1	58	240
35	Gujarati sambaro	cabbage, carrots, corn oil	37.8	3.2	35.2	16.7	393	1622
36	Punjabi cabbage/potato	cabbage, onions, old pots, tomato, butter ghee	75.9	2.1	9.8	8.3	128	530
37	Punjabi cabbage/peas/potato	cabbage, peas, potatoes, veg. oil, tomatoes	73.4	3.3	10.5	8.4	139	576
38	Punjabi cauliflower	cauliflower, onions, veg. oil	78.9	3.4	8.9	4.1	107	441
39	Punjabi cauliflower/potato	cauliflower, old pots, onions, butter	71.8	4.0	7.0	12.8	126	527
40	Punjabi cauliflower/potato/tomato	cauliflower, potatoes, tomatoes, onions, ghee	77.6	3.5	5.8	9.1	100	416
41	Punjabi runner beans/potato	runner beans, potatoes, onions, tomatoes, butter	76.5	2.3	5.7	12.1	105	439
42	Punjabi gourd	bottle gourd, tomatoes, onions, butter ghee, urad	71.3	2.5	13.4	9.1	166	687
43	Punjabi gourd/potato	bottle gourd, potatoes, tomatoes, veg. oil	84.6	0.9	8.1	5.2	96	398
44	Gujarati dhudi	bottle gourd, corn oil	91.0	0.2	6.9	1.4	68	281
45	Punjabi tindora	tinda gourd, tomatoes, corn oil	56.5	2.4	32.3	6.1	323	1333
46	Gujarati tindora	tinda gourd, veg. oil	57.7	2.1	32.8	4.9	319	1316
47	Gujarati turia/potato	ridge gourd, potatoes, tomatoes, veg. oil	83.7	1.3	5.3	7.9	82	341
48	Punjabi karela	karela, spring onions, tomatoes, corn oil	75.4	2.1	14.1	3.8	149	617
49	Gujarati karela	karela, corn oil	89.5	1.0	6.3	0.5	63	259
50	Gujarati guar	raw cluster beans, tomatoes, peanut oil	70.1	2.3	18.1	3.8	186	768
51	Gujarati mooli bhaji (miser)	mooli (radish), veg. oil, chick pea flour	68.5	2.6	13.9	7.2	160	665

Vegetable dishes 34 - 51

Inorganic constituents per 100g

No	Recipe	Na mg	K mg	Ca mg	Mg mg	P mg	Fe mg	Cu mg	Zn mg	Cl mg
34	Punjabi cabbage	8	271	48	9	42	0.7	0.03	0.3	41
35	Gujarati sambaro	42	611	107	15	78	1.4	0.06	0.6	97
36	Punjabi cabbage/potato	14	339	44	12	48	0.8	0.04	0.3	64
37	Punjabi cabbage/peas/potato	5	314	33	16	63	1.2	0.04	0.5	45
38	Punjabi caul flower	21	377	26	17	64	0.8	0.04	0.6	48
39	Punjabi caul flower/potato	71	505	23	23	74	0.8	0.08	0.7	152
40	Punjabi caul flower/potato/tomato	20	450	24	20	64	0.8	0.1	0.5	69
41	Punjabi runner beans/potato	60	357	27	21	46	1.0	0.07	0.3	138
42	Punjabi gourd	26	325	36	23	51	1.1	0.11	0.9	65
43	Punjabi gourd/potato	6	165	12	9	19	0.4	0.04	0.5	25
44	Gujarati dhudi	1	61	9	5	7	0.3	0.02	0.4	3
45	Punjabi tindora	59	169	39	23	42	1.4	0.18	**0.6**	91
46	Gujarati tindora	49	60	41	23	38	1.9	0.18	**0.6**	60
47	Gujarati turia/potato	13	240	11	16	33	0.4	0.09	0.2	61
48	Punjabi karela	7	410	31	31	53	1.9	0.23	0.5	44
49	Gujarati karela	1	211	12	20	31	0.9	0.17	0.3	13
50	Gujarati guar	18	324	98	49	43	1.8	0.11	0.6	57
51	Gujarati mooli bhaji (miser)	958	344	52	35	60	1.4	0.06	0.6	1470

Vegetable dishes 34 - 51

Vitamin content per 100g

No	Recipe	REQ ug	Vit. D ug	Vit. E mg	Vit. B1 mg	Vit. B2 mg	Niacin mg	Vit. B6 mg	Vit. B12 ug	Folate ug	Vit. C mg
34	Punjabi cabbage	52	0	0.69	0.13	0.02	0.8	0.16	0	31	19
35	Gujarati sambaro	1990	0	6.97	0.28	0.03	1.2	0.34	0	60	38
36	Punjabi cabbage/potato	139	0.2	0.73	0.14	0.02	0.9	0.21	0	32	20
37	Punjabi cabbage/peas/potato	51	0	0.25	0.22	0.02	1.3	0.17	0	29	16
38	Punjabi cauliflower	53	0	0.25	0.14	0.04	1.3	0.22	0	29	19
39	Punjabi cauliflower/potato	85	0.1	0.38	0.21	0.04	1.5	0.38	0	35	19
40	Punjabi cauliflower/potato/tomato	56	0.1	0.7	0.19	0.04	1.67	0.36	0	54	34
41	Punjabi runner beans/potato	88	0.1	0.44	0.14	0.02	0.8	0.25	0	26	8
42	Punjabi gourd	123	0.3	N	0.10	0.03	1.1	N	0	11	6
43	Punjabi gourd/potato	5	0	N	0.05	0.02	0.4	N	0	5	3
44	Gujarati dhudi	2	0	N	0.02	0.01	0.2	N	0	2	1
45	Punjabi tindora	21	0	N	0.06	0.09	0.8	N	0	29	15
46	Gujarati tindora	4	0	N	0.05	0.09	0.6	N	0	80	12
47	Gujarati turia/potato	16	0	N	0.09	0.02	0.6	N	0	16	4
48	Punjabi karela	106	0	N	0.09	0.04	1.0	0.10	0	28	73
49	Gujarati karela	36	0	1.07	0.05	0.02	0.4	N	0	14	59
50	Gujarati guar	16	0	3.25	0.14	0.07	0.9	0.05	0	2	3
51	Gujarati mooli bhaji (miser)	19	0	0.23	0.06	0.04	0.9	0.10	0	28	13

Pulse Dishes

Pulse dishes 52 - 68

Composition of food per 100g

No	Recipe	Main Ingredients	Water g	Protein g	Fat g	CHO g	Energy kcals	Energy kj
52	Punjabi peas/potato	peas, potatoes, tomatoes, onions, butter	84.1	2.3	5.2	6.1	79	327
53	Gujarati peas/potato	peas, potato, tomatoes veg. oil	74.3	3.3	9.7	9.8	136	566
54	Punjabi masoor/tomato dhal	split red lentils, onion, tomatoes, butter, green chilli	78.7	4.4	4.5	10.6	97	408
55	Punjabi masoor dhal	split red lentils, onions, corn oil	69.7	6.7	4.6	16.6	130	547
56	Punjabi masoor dhal - thick	split red lentils, butter ghee,	37.3	15.8	4.4	37.4	243	1030
57	Punjabi masoor/mung dhal	split red lentils, mung beans, butter, tomato, onion	74.0	6.0	4.6	12.5	112	470
58	Punjabi masoor/mung/channa dhal	split red lentils, mung, chickpeas, onion, butter ghee	60.4	9.6	4.6	20.6	156	658
59	Pakistani masoor dhal	split red lentils, butter ghee	70.1	6.2	6.3	14.5	135	566
60	Bengali masoor dhal	split red lentils, onions, corn oil,	79.7	4.0	2.8	9.7	77	325
61	Punjabi channa dhal - thin	split chick peas, onions, butter ghee	71.1	6.4	3.1	15.2	110	465
62	Punjabi channa dhal - thick	split chick peas, butter ghee, onions	42.1	13.1	10.2	28.8	252	1061
63	Punjabi channa/tomato	split chick peas, tomatoes, onions, corn oil	77.1	4.5	5.6	10.5	108	451
64	Punjabi chickpeas	whole chick peas, onions, coriander, corn oil, tom. puree	53.0	10.3	5.1	24.6	179	755
65	Punjabi channa aloo	whole chick peas, onions, potatoes, tomatoes, corn oil	44.7	9.1	11.8	27.5	246	1031
66	Punjabi channa/urad dhal	split chick peas, urad gram, onions, butter	78.3	5.1	3.2	9.8	86	363
67	Pakistani channa dhal	split chick peas, tomatoes, onions, butter ghee	73.3	5.1	6.2	11.6	119	500
68	Pakistani chickpea curry	whole chick peas, potatoes, tomatoes, corn oil	69.0	4.4	9.3	12.9	149	623

Pulse dishes 52 - 68

Composition of food per 100g

No	Recipe	PUFA g	MUFA g	SFA g	Chol mg	Starch g	Sugar g	NSP g
52	Punjabi peas/potato	0.4	1.2	3.2	13	4.0	1.5	1.6
53	Gujarati peas/potato	4.6	3.3	1.1	0	7.3	1.7	2.2
54	Punjabi masoor/tomato dhal	0.2	1.1	2.8	12	9.0	0.9	1.0
55	Punjabi masoor dhal	2.6	1.1	0.6	0	13.8	1.6	1.6
56	Punjabi masoor dhal - thick	0.5	1.0	2.5	10	33.8	1.6	3.3
57	Punjabi masoor/mung dhal	0.3	1.1	2.9	12	10.7	0.9	**1.8**
58	Punjabi masoor/mung/channa dhal	0.5	1.0	2.5	11	17.4	1.6	**3.3**
59	Pakistani masoor dhal	0.4	1.5	4.0	17	13.1	0.6	1.3
60	Bengali masoor dhal	1.6	0.7	0.4	0	8.3	0.8	0.9
61	Punjabi charna dhal - thin	0.9	0.7	1.1	4	13.0	1.1	3.2
62	Punjabi charna dhal - thick	1.8	2.4	5.0	20	25.2	1.7	**6.2**
63	Punjabi charna/tomato	3.2	1.3	0.7	0	8.3	1.4	2.2
64	Punjabi chickpeas	2.7	1.1	0.6	0	20.5	2.3	**5.1**
65	Punjabi charna aloo	6.7	2.8	1.4	0	21.6	4.1	5.0
66	Punjabi charna/urad dhal	0.4	0.7	1.7	7	8.5	0.7	**2.6**
67	Pakistani channa dhal	0.8	1.4	3.4	14	9.5	1.3	1.8
68	Pakistani chickpea curry	5.2	2.2	1.1	0	10.3	1.8	2.3

29

Pulse dishes 52 - 68

Inorganic constituents per 100g

No	Recipe	Na mg	K mg	Ca mg	Mg mg	P mg	Fe mg	Cu mg	Zn mg	Cl mg
52	Punjabi peas/potato	52	177	10	13	45	0.9	0.03	0.4	101
53	Gujarati peas/potato	13	287	12	20	62	1.2	0.06	0.5	58
54	Punjabi masoor/tomato dhal	46	153	12	16	63	1.4	0.11	0.6	75
55	Punjabi masoor dhal	10	223	18	23	93	2.1	0.17	0.9	22
56	Punjabi masoor dhal - thick	25	476	34	55	213	5.1	0.38	2.1	45
57	Punjabi masoor/mung dhal	48	250	12	26	86	1.6	0.14	0.7	77
58	Punjabi masoor/mung/channa dhal	17	413	22	42	138	2.6	0.27	1.2	32
59	Pakistani masoor dhal	121	205	18	24	87	2.2	0.16	0.8	191
60	Bengali masoor dhal	503	142	12	18	57	1.4	0.10	0.5	779
61	Punjabi channa dhal - thin	12	311	48	39	94	1.7	0.28	0.9	20
62	Punjabi channa dhal - thick	23	575	30	63	190	3.1	0.59	2.1	37
63	Punjabi channa/tomato	13	239	13	23	67	1.1	0.21	0.7	26
64	Punjabi chickpeas	25	535	83	63	152	2.7	0.46	1.5	66
65	Punjabi channa aloo	33	630	71	58	142	2.4	0.40	1.3	86
66	Punjabi channa/urad dhal	34	202	23	29	76	1.3	0.19	0.7	N
67	Pakistani channa dhal	369	263	15	28	77	1.3	0.23	0.8	576
68	Pakistani chickpea curry	332	283	34	28	54	1.8	0.17	0.7	530

Pulse dishes 52 - 68

Vitamin content per 100g

No	Recipe	REQ ug	Vit. D ug	Vit. E mg	Vit. B1 mg	Vit. B2 mg	Niacin mg	Vit. B6 mg	Vit. B12 ug	Folate ug	Vit. C mg
52	Punjabi peas/potato	77	0.1	0.34	0.18	0.01	1.0	0.10	0	12	5
53	Gujarati peas/potato	27	0	0.42	0.26	0.02	1.4	0.16	0	17	7
54	Punjabi masoor/tomato dhal	53	0.1	0.18	0.08	0.03	0.9	0.10	0	4	2
55	Punjabi masoor dhal	3	0	N	0.13	0.04	1.3	0.16	0	6	Tr
56	Punjabi masoor dhal - thick	34	0.1	N	0.26	0.10	2.8	0.32	0	12	Tr
57	Punjabi masoor/mung dhal	55	0.1	N	0.09	0.04	1.1	0.10	0	11	1
58	Punjabi masoor/mung/channa dhal	56	0.1	N	0.14	0.07	1.8	0.18	0	22	1
59	Pakistani masoor dhal	48	0.1	0.2	0.10	0.04	1.1	0.13	0	5	Tr
60	Bengali masoor dhal	2	0	0.46	0.07	0.02	0.8	0.09	0	4	1
61	Punjabi channa dhal - thin	14	Tr	0.9	0.10	0.06	1.2	0.14	0	27	Tr
62	Punjabi channa dhal - thick	59	0.2	1.9	0.18	0.11	2.3	0.25	0	52	Tr
63	Punjabi channa/tomato	7	0	1.52	0.07	0.04	0.9	0.10	0	18	1
64	Punjabi chickpeas	17	0	1.91	0.17	0.10	2.0	0.23	0	44	2
65	Punjabi channa aloo	19	0	3.16	0.22	0.08	2.2	0.36	0	41	5
66	Punjabi channa/urad dhal	38	Tr	N	0.07	0.06	1.0	**0.10**	0	17	Tr
67	Pakistani channa dhal	57	0.1	0.92	0.08	0.04	1.0	0.11	0	21	1
68	Pakistani chickpea curry	12	0	2.14	0.09	0.03	1.0	0.15	0	16	3

31

Pulse dishes 69 - 85

Composition of food per 100g

No	Recipe	Main Ingredients	Water g	Protein g	Fat g	CHO g	Energy kcals	Energy kj
69	Punjabi mung dhal	mung beans, onions, butter ghee, coriander,	.77.0	5.9	3.0	10.6	90	380
70	Punjabi whole mung dhal	mung beans whole, onions, butter	81.8	3.8	3.6	7.7	77	322
71	Punjabi whole mung curry	mung beans whole, tomatoes, corn oil, onions	77.6	3.6	8.4	7.5	118	491
72	Punjabi mung/masoor dhal	mung beans, split red lentils, onions, butter ghee	77.7	5.4	3.4	10.6	91	381
73	Gujarati whole mung curry	mung beans whole, tomatoes, onions, butter ghee	73.1	5.2	5.8	11.2	115	481
74	Pakistani mung dhal	mung beans, veg. oil, onions	76.7	5.3	5.1	9.2	101	421
75	Ismaili whole mung curry	mung beans whole, onions, tomatoes, sunfl. oil,	76.0	4.2	5.9	8.1	98	410
76	Punjabi urad dhal	urad (black gram),onions, butter ghee	87.0	2.5	3.4	5.0	60	249
77	Punjabi urad/tomato dhal	urad (black gram),tomatoes, onions, butter	78.6	4.5	4.4	8.2	90	377
78	Punjabi mung/moth dhal	urad gram, mung beans, veg. margarine, onions	74.9	5.5	5.6	9.4	107	448
79	Punjabi whole moth dhal	urad gram (whole), tomatoes, onions, butter ghee	80.6	4.4	3.9	7.5	82	343
80	Pakistani dhal maash	urad gram, onions, veg. oil,	69.1	6.9	5.5	11.9	123	517
81	Punjabi toor dhal	pigeon peas, tomatoes, veg. oil	79.6	3.9	4.6	10.4	96	402
82	Gujarati tuwar dhal	pigeon peas, tomatoes, corn oil	83.0	3.8	1.5	10.2	67	284
83	Gujarati pigeon pea dhal	pigeon peas whole, aubergine, veg. oil	61.4	4.9	16.1	14.3	218	908
84	Ismaili dhal/dar	pigeon peas, split red lentils, tomatoes, veg. oil	81.5	4.1	2.1	9.9	69	294
85	Punjabi soya beans dhal	soya beans, onions, butter ghee, tomatoes	61.1	11.6	13.3	6.8	192	798

Pulse dishes 69 - 85

Composition of food per 100g

No	Recipe	PUFA g	MUFA g	SFA g	Chol mg	Starch g	Sugar g	NSP g
69	Punjabi mung dhal	0.2	0.7	1.9	8	8.7	0.9	**2.3**
70	Punjabi whole mung dhal	0.2	0.8	2.3	10	6.5	0.6	1.6
71	Punjabi whole mung curry	4.8	2.1	1.1	0	5.8	1.0	**2.9**
72	Punjabi munj/masoor dhal	0.2	0.8	2.1	9	9.0	0.7	**3.0**
73	Gujarati whole mung curry	0.3	1.4	3.7	15	8.3	1.9	2.4
74	Pakistani mung dhal	2.4	1.7	0.6	0	8.2	0.4	**2.2**
75	Ismaili whole mung curry	3.6	1.2	0.7	0	5.6	1.7	1.7
76	Punjabi urad dhal	0.2	0.8	2.1	9	3.5	1.0	**0.9**
77	Punjabi urad/tomato dhal	0.3	1.0	2.8	12	6.8	0.9	**1.6**
78	Punjabi mung/moth dhal	1.5	2.0	1.6	1	8.2	0.6	**2.0**
79	Punjabi whole moth dhal	0.3	0.9	2.5	10	6.0	1.1	**1.6**
80	Pakistani dhal maash	2.6	1.8	0.6	0	10.0	1.0	**2.3**
81	Punjabi toor dhal	2.2	1.5	0.5	0	9.5	0.6	**2.0**
82	Gujarati tuwar dhal	0.8	0.3	0.2	0	9.4	0.5	**0.9**
83	Gujarati pigeon pea dhal	7.8	5.6	1.7	0	12.8	1.0	**2.6**
84	Ismaili dhal/dar	0.9	0.7	0.2	0	8.8	0.7	**0.8**
85	Punjabi soya beans dhal	3.1	2.9	5.6	21	1.8	2.9	5.3

33

Pulse dishes 69 - 85

Inorganic constituents per 100g

No	Recipe	Na mg	K mg	Ca mg	Mg mg	P mg	Fe mg	Cu mg	Zn mg	Cl mg
69	Punjabi mung dhal	7	299	11	29	87	1.3	0.13	0.6	13
70	Punjabi whole mung dhal	35	213	17	24	60	1.0	0.08	0.4	54
71	Punjabi whole mung curry	7	227	17	23	54	0.9	0.08	0.4	17
72	Punjabi mung/masoor dhal	11	237	12	24	78	1.4	0.12	0.6	18
73	Gujarati whole mung curry	17	357	25	34	82	1.4	0.12	0.6	40
74	Pakistani mung dhal	171	264	9	28	79	1.2	0.11	0.5	262
75	Ismaili whole mung curry	956	275	18	31	67	1.2	0.12	0.5	1483
76	Punjabi urad dhal	5	101	17	16	38	0.6	0.07	0.3	6
77	Punjabi urad/tomato dhal	50	184	29	29	71	1.2	0.13	0.5	N
78	Punjabi mung/moth dhal	66	241	23	32	83	1.4	0.14	0.6	94
79	Punjabi whole moth dhal	15	178	27	27	64	1.1	0.13	0.5	22
80	Pakistani dhal maash	17	276	50	48	107	1.9	0.21	0.8	N
81	Punjabi toor dhal	12	265	8	16	56	0.5	0.17	0.4	12
82	Gujarati tuwar dhal	7	253	7	15	55	0.5	0.16	0.4	4
83	Gujarati pigeon pea dhal	9	384	36	26	72	0.9	0.29	0.6	5
84	Ismaili dhal/dar	151	238	16	19	61	1.1	0.15	0.5	232
85	Punjabi soya beans dhal	4	588	81	80	215	3.2	0.50	1.4	13

No	Recipe	REQ ug	Vit. D ug	Vit. E mg	Vit.B1 mg	Vit.B2 mg	Niacin mg	Vit. B6 mg	Vit. B12 ug	Folate ug	Vit. C mg
69	Punjabi mung dhal	31	0.1	N	0.07	0.05	1.1	0.08	0	16	1
70	Punjabi whole mung dhal	40	Tr	N	0.05	0.03	0.8	0.06	0	11	Tr
71	Punjabi whole mung curry	7	0	N	0.05	0.03	0.8	0.07	0	11	1
72	Punjabi mung/masoor dhal	46	0.1	N	0.07	0.04	1.0	0.09	0	11	Tr
73	Gujarati whole mung curry	56	0.1	0.65	0.08	0.05	1.3	0.11	0	17	2
74	Pakistani mung dhal	15	0	N	0.06	0.04	1.0	0.06	0	14	Tr
75	Ismaili whole mung curry	20	0	N	0.06	0.04	1.0	0.09	0	12	2
76	Punjabi urad dhal	26	0.1	N	0.05	0.02	0.6	N	0	7	Tr
77	Punjabi urad/tomato dhal	56	0.1	N	0.07	0.05	1.0	N	0	12	1
78	Punjabi mung/moth dhal	92	0.5	0.01	0.07	0.06	1.1	0.04	0	14	Tr
79	Punjabi whole moth dhal	34	0.1	N	0.06	0.05	1.0	N	0	12	1
80	Pakistani dhal maash	26	0	N	0.10	0.09	1.6	N	0	18	Tr
81	Punjabi toor dhal	6	0	N	0.12	0.02	0.6	N	0	9	1
82	Gujarati tuwar dhal	7	0	N	0.12	0.02	0.6	N	0	9	1
83	Gujarati pigeon pea dhal	5	0	N	0.17	0.02	0.8	N	0	14	1
84	Ismaili dhal/bar	7	0	N	0.10	0.02	0.7	N	0	7	1
85	Punjabi soya beans dhal	61	0.2	1.24	0.18	0.07	2.2	0.13	0	60	1

Pulse dishes 86 - 92

Composition of food per 100g

No	Recipe	Main Ingredients	Water g	Protein g	Fat g	CHO g	Energy kcals	Energy kj
86	Punjabi khadi	yogurt, butter ghee, chick pea flour	81.8	3.0	8.7	5.2	110	456
87	Gujarati kahdi	buttermilk, chick pea flour, butter ghee	86.8	2.3	2.2	8.6	61	258
88	Ismaili khadi	low fat yogurt, onions, chick pea flour, veg. oil	87.7	2.6	3.1	4.4	49	206
89	Pakistani khadi	low fat yogurt, onions, corn oil, chick pea flour	66.4	5.0	12.7	10.4	170	705
90	Punjabi kitchadi	basmati rice, mung beans, butter	75.8	4.3	2.2	15.7	99	414
91	Gujarati khichadi	mung beans, butter ghee, white rice	71.2	5.0	8.8	12.4	147	612
92	Ismaili kitchadi.	white rice, mung beans, veg. margarine	79.8	2.5	1.6	15.1	81	343

No	Recipe	PUFA g	MUFA g	SFA g	Chol mg	Starch g	Sugar g	NSP g
86	Punjabi khadi	0.4	2.2	5.5	25	2.0	3.0	0.5
87	Gujarati kahdi	0.2	0.5	1.4	6	1.3	7.2	0.3
88	Ismaili khadi	1.0	1.1	0.8	4	1.6	2.6	0.4
89	Pakistani khadi	7.0	3.2	1.8	2	4.9	4.8	1.4
90	Punjabi kitchadi	0.1	0.5	1.3	6	15.0	0.2	1.3
91	Gujarati khichadi	0.4	2.1	5.7	24	11.5	0.3	1.7
92	Ismaili kitchadi	0.0	0.0	0.0	0	14.7	0.1	0.6

Pulse dishes 86 - 92

Inorganic constituents per 100g

No	Recipe	Na mg	K mg	Ca mg	Mg mg	P mg	Fe mg	Cu mg	Zn mg	Cl mg
86	Punjabi khadi	33	152	82	13	78	0.4	0.03	0.4	70
87	Gujarati kahdi	27	101	60	10	54	0.3	0.02	0.3	43
88	Ismaili khadi	295	125	65	14	58	0.7	0.03	0.3	468
89	Pakistani khadi	641	289	124	30	124	1.3	0.10	0.7	1000
90	Punjabi kitchadi	20	170	7	18	58	0.9	0.09	0.5	32
91	Gujarati khichadi	2	212	7	22	70	1.0	0.09	0.4	4
92	Ismaili kitchadi	374	91	3	12	38	0.4	0.06	0.3	578

Vitamin content per 100g

No	Recipe	REQ ug	Vit. D ug	Vit. E mg	Vit. B1 mg	Vit. B2 mg	Niacin mg	Vit. B6 mg	Vit. B12 ug	Folate ug	Vit. C mg
86	Punjabi khadi	69	0.2	0.39	0.03	0.09	0.6	0.05	0.1	7	Tr
87	Gujarati kahdi	16	Tr	0.15	0.02	0.07	0.5	0.01	0.1	6	0
88	Ismaili khadi	13	Tr	0.11	0.03	0.07	0.6	0.05	Tr	5	1
89	Pakistani khadi	36	0	2.35	0.07	0.12	1.1	0.11	0.1	15	1
90	Punjabi kitchadi	22	Tr	N	0.03	0.02	0.4	0.05	0	10	0
91	Gujarati khichadi	66	0.2	0.28	0.05	0.03	0.8	0.05	0	12	0
92	Ismaili kitchadi	16	0.1	0.15	0.02	0.02	0.6	0.06	0	6	0

Rice and Cereal Dishes

Rice and cereal dishes 93 - 112

Composition of food per 100g

No	Recipe	Main Ingredients	Water g	Protein g	Fat g	CHO g	Energy kcals	Energy kj
93	Punjabi meat pilau	basmati rice, lamb, corn oil	50.1	7.8	15.4	28.5	277	1157
94	Bengali meat pilau	bas. rice, onions, lamb, new pots, veg. oil, butter ghee	54.5	4.5	13.6	25.6	244	1013
95	Ismaili meat pilau (ukni)	lamb, basmati rice, old pots, onions, sun9l. oil	66.9	6.2	8.1	16.8	165	685
96	Pakistani meat pilau	lamb breast, basmati rice, onions, corn oil	55.3	7.0	16.1	20.0	253	1050
97	Punjabi chicken biryani	basmati rice, chicken, onions, corn oil	61.8	7.3	6.3	23.7	182	760
98	Ismaili chicken pilau (ukni)	chicken, basmati rice, onions, tomatoes, sunfl. oil	67.5	7.7	4.0	19.0	143	599
99	Ismaili biryani	chicken, basmati rice, onions, tomatoes, yogurt	57.8	12.8	4.5	22.7	183	766
100	Punjabi peas pilau	basmati rice, peas, ghee, onions	63.3	3.7	6.8	24.2	173	721
101	Punjabi mixed veg. pilau	basmati rice, peas, carrots, butter, onions	62.0	3.3	7.5	25.0	181	754
102	Pakistani veg. pilau	basmati rice, peas, onions, veg. oil	54.9	4.3	3.0	35.4	187	782
103	Ismaili rice	white rice, sunfl. oil	72.1	1.9	4.3	20.4	129	538
104	Bengali rice pitta	rice flour	74.9	1.8	0.2	22.6	103	432
105	Punjabi paratha	white chapati flour, water, butter ghee	39.1	6.1	6.2	48.5	262	1110
106	Pakistani paratha	white chapati flour, water, veg. oil	35.9	5.7	12.2	45.4	303	1274
107	Punjabi methi paratha	brown chapati flour, fenugreek leaves, water, corn oil	45.5	7.2	2.8	41.2	208	882
108	Bengali paratha	white chapati flour, water, butter ghee, veg. oil	35.6	4.6	23.1	36.0	361	1507
109	Pakistani roti	brown chapati flour, water	37.2	8.2	0.9	52.8	238	1016
110	Ismaili rotli	brown chapati flour, water, sunfl. oil	24.1	8.6	10.9	55.2	339	1432
111	Bengali chapati	white chapati flour, water	36.4	7.1	0.4	56.1	242	1031
112	Ismaili dhokra	buttermilk, semolina, sunfl. oil, coriander leaves	63.0	5.3	4.5	26.9	162	686

Rice and cereal dishes 93 - 112

Composition of food per 100g

No	Recipe	PUFA g	MUFA g	SFA g	Chol mg	Starch g	Sugar g	NSP g
93	Punjabi meat pilau	2.4	5.5	6.5	27	28.5	0.0	0.2
94	Bengali meat pilau	3.5	4.1	5.0	24	24.5	0.8	0.4
95	Ismaili meat pilau (ukni)	2.3	2.5	2.7	19	16.1	0.5	0.4
96	Pakistani meat pilau	3.7	5.5	6.0	23	19.2	0.5	0.3
97	Punjabi chicken biryani	3.1	1.7	1.0	14	23.3	0.3	0.2
98	Ismaili chicken pilau (ukni)	2.1	1.0	0.6	11.3	18.5	0.4	11.3
99	Ismaili biryani	1.5	1.6	1.0	29	20.8	1.6	0.5
100	Punjabi peas pilau	0.4	1.6	4.2	18	22.7	0.9	1.4
101	Punjabi mixed veg. pilau	0.4	1.7	4.7	19	23.2	1.4	1.3
102	Pakistani veg. pilau	1.4	0.9	0.3	0	34.1	0.8	1.3
103	Ismaili rice	2.6	0.8	0.5	0	20.4	0.0	0.1
104	Bengali rice pitta	0.0	0.0	0.0	0	22.6	0.0	0.6
105	Punjabi paratha	0.3	1.4	4.0	17	47.2	1.3	1.9
106	Pakistani paratha	5.9	4.2	1.3	0	44.2	1.2	1.9
107	Punjabi methi paratha	1.5	0.6	0.4	0	38.5	1.8	5.4
108	Bengali paratha	6.0	6.8	8.8	32	35.1	1.0	1.4
109	Pakistani roti	0.4	0.1	0.1	0	50.5	2.3	4.5
110	Ismaili rotli	6.7	2.1	1.3	0	52.8	2.4	4.8
111	Bengali chapati	0.1	0.0	0.1	0	54.6	1.5	2.2
112	Ismaili dhokra	2.3	0.8	0.6	1	23.9	2.9	0.8

Rice and cereal dishes 93 - 112

Inorganic constituents per 100g

No	Recipe	Na mg	K mg	Ca mg	Mg mg	P mg	Fe mg	Cu mg	Zn mg	Cl mg
93	Punjabi meat pilau	35	122	4	10	84	0.6	0.11	1.5	34
94	Bengali meat pilau	342	91	12	8	47	0.7	0.09	0.8	529
95	Ismaili meat pilau (ukni)	363	175	12	15	66	1.0	0.09	1.0	567
96	Pakistani meat pilau	265	103	15	9	67	1.0	0.10	1.3	387
97	Punjabi chicken biryani	22	123	10	10	73	0.6	0.10	0.7	29
98	Ismaili chicken pilau (ukni)	377	147	11	13	79	0.5	0.05	0.5	577
99	Ismaili biryani	128	263	27	17	134	1.0	0.17	1.0	182
100	Punjabi peas pilau	3	118	11	12	53	1.1	0.06	0.6	14
101	Punjabi mixed veg. pilau	70	120	15	7	48	0.9	0.02	0.5	21
102	Pakistani veg. pilau	225	93	16	13	50	0.9	0.08	0.2	359
103	Ismaili rice	325	28	5	6	19	0.3	0.05	0.3	506
104	Bengali rice pitta	56	68	7	7	37	0.5	0.06	0.4	85
105	Punjabi paratha	9	125	52	18	87	1.6	0.16	0.8	44
106	Pakistani paratha	273	117	49	19	82	1.5	0.15	0.8	447
107	Punjabi methi paratha	852	159	76	56	146	3.6	0.23	1.2	1328
108	Bengali paratha	285	93	39	16	65	1.2	0.12	0.6	463
109	Pakistani roti	28	200	62	49	179	2.4	0.24	1.5	48
110	Ismaili rotli	68	210	64	52	187	2.6	0.25	1.6	110
111	Bengali chapati	11	145	61	21	101	1.8	0.18	0.9	49
112	Ismaili dhokra	136	172	71	20	87	1.0	0.06	0.5	239

Rice and Cereal dishes 93 - 112

Vitamin content per 100g

No	Recipe	REQ ug	Vit. D ug	Vit. E mg	Vit. B1 mg	Vit. B2 mg	Niacin mg	Vit. B6 ug	Vit. B12 ug	Folate ug	Vit. C mg
93	Punjabi meat pilau	0	Tr	1.28	0.38	0.45	2.9	0.11	0.3	4	0
94	Bengali meat pilau	46	0.1	0.25	0.04	0.02	0.8	0.11	0.2	2	1
95	Ismaili meat pilau (ukni)	1	Tr	1.67	0.05	0.04	1.5	0.11	0.5	5	1
96	Pakistani meat pilau	1	Tr	1.06	0.04	0.04	1.4	0.08	0.3	1	Tr
97	Punjabi chicken biryani	0	Tr	0.95	0.04	0.03	1.7	0.12	0	5	Tr
98	Ismaili chicken pilau (ukni)	2	Tr	1.56	0.05	0.03	3.1	0.16	Tr	1	Tr
99	Ismaili biryani	13	Tr	0.24	0.06	0.07	3.6	0.20	Tr	6	2
100	Punjabi peas pilau	61	0.1	0.3	0.13	0.01	0.6	0.07	0	11	3
101	Punjabi mixed veg. pilau	200	0.1	0.42	0.09	0.01	0.4	0.07	0	10	2
102	Pakistani veg. pilau	17	0	0.09	0.06	0.02	0.4	0.09	0	12	2
103	Ismaili rice	0	0	2.08	0.01	0.01	0.8	0.05	0	3	0
104	Bengali rice pitta	0	0	0.03	0.02	0.01	0.9	0.05	0	Tr	0
105	Punjabi paratha	45	0.1	0.38	0.22	0.04	2.4	0.11	0	12	0
106	Pakistani paratha	0	0	0.18	0.16	0.03	2.2	0.08	0	6	0
107	Punjabi metni paratha	181	0	1.13	0.17	0.11	3.7	0.18	0	62	18
108	Bengali paratha	87	0.2	0.52	0.13	0.03	1.7	0.06	0	5	0
109	Pakistani roti	0	0	0.43	0.14	0.03	4.2	0.16	0	10	0
110	Ismaili rotli	0	0	5.37	0.14	0.03	4.4	0.17	0	11	0
111	Bengali chapati	0	0	0.22	0.20	0.03	2.7	0.09	0	7	0
112	Ismaili dhokra	8	0	1.80	0.05	0.10	1.3	0.09	0.1	10	1

Meat Dishes

Meat dishes 113 - 130

Composition of food per 100g

No	Recipe	Main Ingredients	Water g	Protein g	Fat g	CHO g	Energy kcals	Energy kj
113	Punjabi lamb curry	lamb shoulder, onions, veg. oil, tomatoes	71.3	5.9	18.4	3.1	201	831
114	Punjabi lamb/potato curry	lamb leg, old potatoes, onions, vegetable oil	63.3	14.8	14.6	6.3	214	889
115	Punjabi mutton curry	mutton, onions, butter ghee	72.2	6.8	19.0	1.5	204	842
116	Punjabi lamb chops	lamb chops, tomatoes, onions, sunfl. oil	48.1	13.2	35.9	1.6	382	1579
117	Ismaili lamb curry	lamb, tomatoes, onions, veg. oil	75.0	12.3	8.8	1.8	133	556
118	Pakistani lamb curry	lamb breast, tomatoes, onions, corn oil, yogurt	59.7	9.1	25.9	2.6	276	1142
119	Bengali lamb curry	lamb, onions, corn oil	60.2	16.1	17.4	2.8	229	953
120	Punjabi lamb keema	lamb mince, onions, corn oil	54.6	11.9	30.0	2.5	327	1351
121	Punjabi matar keema	lamb mince, onions, tomatoes, margarine, peas	67.4	10.0	17.3	3.8	210	868
122	Ismaili lamb keema	lamb mince, tomatoes, onions, tomato puree	75.9	6.8	13.7	2.0	158	653
123	Pakistani lamb keema	lamb mince, onions, sunfl. oil, tomatoes	60.0	6.3	26.8	3.2	275	1133
124	Pakistani matar keema	lamb mince, onions, peas, tomatoes, veg. ghee	59.3	14.4	16.9	5.1	227	944
125	Pakistani aloo keema	beef mince, old potatoes, onions, tomatoes	60.7	11.4	15.9	9.1	222	923
126	Bengali lamb keema	lamb mince, onions, veg. oil	51.3	12.3	29.1	3.1	320	1324
127	Punjabi lamb kebab	lamb, onions	64.1	15.7	15.8	3.2	217	900
128	Pakistani aloo gosht	lamb leg, onions, old potatoes, sunfl. oil	68.2	8.9	12.4	7.6	174	724
129	Pakistani kofta	lamb mince, onions, sunfl. oil, tomatoes	60.0	10.2	24.3	2.5	268	1106
130	Pakistani gosht palak	lamb leg, spinach, tomatoes, coriander seeds	75.1	9.5	9.4	2.0	126	523

Meat dishes 113 - 130

Composition of food per 100g

No	Recipe	PUFA g	MUFA g	SFA g	Chol mg	Starch g	Sugar g	NSP g
113	Punjabi lamb curry	4.8	6.8	5.6	23	0.5	2.0	0.6
114	Punjabi lamb/potato curry	0.7	5.6	7.2	60	5.0	1.0	0.6
115	Punjabi mutton curry	0.8	5.6	11.4	63	0.1	1.0	0.3
116	Punjabi lamb chops	4.5	12.9	16.0	68	0.4	1.0	0.3
117	Ismaili lamb curry	2.0	3.3	2.8	44	0.5	1.0	0.4
118	Pakistani lamb curry	5.9	9.0	9.9	39	0.7	1.6	0.4
119	Bengali lamb curry	6.4	5.1	4.5	58	0.3	1.4	0.4
120	Punjabi lamb keema	4.9	11.0	12.8	53	0.5	1.4	0.5
121	Punjabi matar keema	1.4	6.7	8.1	41	0.6	2.4	0.8
122	Ismaili lamb keema	1.2	5.3	6.6	29	0.3	1.6	0.4
123	Pakistani lamb keema	11.1	7.3	6.8	24	0.4	2.1	0.6
124	Pakistani matar keema	N	N	N	55	1.5	2.5	1.4
125	Pakistani aloo keema	5.0	5.5	4.5	35	7.0	1.7	1.1
126	Bengali lamb keema	3.5	11.3	12.7	54	0.5	1.5	0.6
127	Punjabi lamb kebab	0.8	6.0	7.8	65	0.4	2.0	0.5
128	Pakistani aloo gosht	3.2	3.9	4.4	32	4.2	2.0	0.8
129	Pakistani ko'ta	9.5	6.7	6.6	41	0.3	1.4	0.4
130	Pakistani gosht palak	0.9	3.6	4.2	34	0.1	1.5	0.9

Meat dishes 113 - 130

Inorganic constituents per 100g

No	Recipe	Na mg	K mg	Ca mg	Mg mg	P mg	Fe mg	Cu mg	Zn mg	Cl mg
113	Punjabi lamb curry	32	198	12	11	64	0.6	0.10	1.1	47
114	Punjabi lamb/potato curry	44	375	10	23	148	1.5	0.14	2.3	68
115	Punjabi mutton curry	23	145	7	9	68	0.7	0.06	1.1	33
116	Punjabi lamb chops	60	264	11	18	132	1.2	0.16	1.9	70
117	Ismaili lamb curry	268	284	16	21	120	1.4	0.12	2.4	387
118	Pakistani lamb curry	349	253	24	19	95	1.3	0.11	1.7	510
119	Bengali lamb curry	689	353	26	30	158	2.1	0.15	3.1	1015
120	Punjabi lamb keema	72	243	12	15	114	1.0	0.12	2.3	65
121	Punjabi matar keema	110	269	14	16	108	1.2	0.10	1.6	168
122	Ismaili lamb keema	121	237	13	14	69	0.8	3.11	1.3	173
123	Pakistani lamb keema	633	213	21	19	73	0.9	0.11	1.2	970
124	Pakistani matar keema	478	397	28	33	155	2.6	0.15	2.3	730
125	Pakistani aloo keema	231	389	18	21	112	1.9	0.13	2.5	363
126	Bengali lamb keema	928	286	36	26	123	2.6	0.17	2.4	1376
127	Punjabi lamb kebab	54	357	20	22	158	1.7	0.14	2.4	67
128	Pakistani aloo gosht	404	372	34	30	101	1.4	0.13	1.4	628
129	Pakistani kofta	589	285	23	26	107	1.3	0.10	1.6	899
130	Pakistani gosht palak	320	325	67	44	104	1.8	0.12	1.6	366

Meat dishes 113 - 130

Vitamin content per 100g

No	Recipe	REQ ug	Vit. D ug	Vit. E mg	Vit. B$_1$ mg	Vit. B$_2$ mg	Niacin mg	Vit. B$_6$ mg	Vit. B$_{12}$ ug	Folate ug	Vit. C mg
113	Punjabi lamb curry	9	Tr	0.40	0.06	0.06	2.2	0.11	0.5	4	2
114	Punjabi lamb/potato curry	2	Tr	0.14	0.07	0.14	3.9	0.16	1.2	8	2
115	Punjabi mutton curry	96	0.2	0.52	0.05	0.07	2.9	0.09	0.6	2	Tr
116	Punjabi lamb chops	6	Tr	2.14	0.04	0.10	3.2	0.09	0.7	3	1
117	Ismaili lamb curry	6	Tr	0.18	0.04	0.11	3.0	0.09	0.9	4	1
118	Pakistani lamb curry	21	Tr	1.45	0.03	0.07	2.1	0.07	0.4	4	2
119	Bengali lamb curry	33	Tr	1.56	0.06	0.15	4.0	0.12	1.2	4	1
120	Punjabi lamb keema	4	Tr	1.06	0.04	0.08	2.7	0.08	0.5	3	1
121	Punjabi matar keema	96	0.8	0.29	0.06	0.09	2.7	0.10	0.8	6	2
122	Ismaili lamb keema	19	Tr	0.82	0.02	0.05	1.6	0.06	0.3	4	3
123	Pakistani lamb keema	23	Tr	6.81	0.04	0.05	1.5	0.07	0.6	4	2
124	Pakistani matar keema	39	Tr	0.59	0.08	0.15	3.9	0.12	1.1	12	3
125	Pakistani aloo keema	22	Tr	3.07	0.06	0.13	2.5	0.19	0.8	11	4
126	Bengali lamb keema	3	Tr	0.15	0.04	0.09	2.8	0.08	0.6	3	1
127	Punjabi lamb kebab	6	Tr	0.18	0.07	0.15	4.2	0.13	1.3	5	3
128	Pakistani aloo gosht	31	Tr	1.88	0.07	0.09	2.4	0.13	0.7	8	3
129	Pakistani kofta	38	Tr	5.79	0.05	0.11	2.8	0.08	0.8	3	1
130	Pakistani gosht palak	238	Tr	0.69	0.04	0.10	2.5	0.09	0.7	3	4

Meat dishes 131-138,   Egg and cheese dishes 139-142

Composition of food per 100g

No	Recipe	Main Ingredients	Water g	Protein g	Fat g	CHO g	Energy kcals	Energy kj
131	Punjabi chicken curry	chicken, onions, tomato, corn oil	˙78.1	13.4	5.7	1.7	111	465
132	Punjabi chicken curry with yogurt	chicken, tomatoes, veg. oil, onions, yogurt	70.8	12.9	13.0	1.8	175	728
133	Pakistani chicken curry	chicken, tomatoes, onions, corn oil	69.3	8.7	15.7	2.6	181	751
134	Bengali chicken curry	chicken, onions, veg. oil, lemons	67.6	15.1	10.5	2.6	163	679
135	Bengali chicken bhuna	chicken, onions, sunfl. oil, coriander	64.5	19.5	10.3	2.0	174	726
136	Ismaili chicken/potato curry	chicken, new pots, tomatoes, onion, corn oil	78.0	10.1	5.3	4.5	104	435
137	Bengali chicken/potato curry	chicken, old potatoes, tomatoes	72.2	12.3	9.6	4.1	150	624
138	Pakistani roast chicken	chicken, yogurt	68.9	23.6	5.1	0.3	140	588
139	Punjabi matar paneer	paneer, onions, peas, tomatoes, butter ghee	46.2	14.9	24.6	9.6	318	1326
140	Punjabi matar paneer/potato	potato, toms, peas, paneer, onions, margarine	81.3	3.5	5.7	7.5	94	393
141	Punjabi palak paneer	spinach, paneer, onions, tomatoes, sunfl. oil, fenugreek	63.6	8.1	20.1	4.1	230	952
142	Bengali egg curry	eggs, onions, corn oil	55.0	10.5	23.9	5.7	275	1137

Meat dishes 131-138   Egg and cheese dishes 139-142

Composition of food per 100g

No	Recipe	PUFA g	MUFA g	SFA g	Chol mg	Starch g	Sugar g	NSP g
131	Punjabi chicken curry	2.2	1.9	1.3	36	0.3	1.1	0.3
132	Punjabi chicken curry with yogurt	5.5	4.8	1.9	34	0.1	1.5	0.3
133	Pakistani chicken curry	8.3	4.2	2.3	22	0.6	1.7	0.4
134	Bengali chicken curry	4.1	3.9	1.8	40	0.3	1.5	0.6
135	Bengali chicken bhuna	4.5	2.9	2.0	52	0.2	1.1	0.4
136	Ismaili chicken/potato curry	2.2	1.6	1.1	26	3.5	0.9	0.4
137	Bengali chicken/potato curry	4.6	2.8	1.7	32	2.8	0.8	0.4
138	Pakistani roast chicken	0.9	2.1	1.6	65	0.1	0.2	0.0
139	Punjabi matar paneer	N	N	N	N	N	N	2.1
140	Punjabi matar paneer/potato	N	N	N	N	N	N	1.2
141	Punjabi palak paneer	N	N	N	N	N	N	1.2
142	Bengali egg curry	9.9	7.4	4.3	286	0.0	3.6	1.0

Meat dishes 131-138 Egg and cheese dishes 139-142

Composition of food per 100g

No	Recipe	Na mg	K mg	Ca mg	Mg mg	P mg	Fe mg	Cu mg	Zn mg	Cl mg
131	Punjabi chicken curry	56	262	11	18	135	0.6	0.14	0.8	64
132	Punjabi chicken curry with yogurt	64	292	18	19	135	0.6	0.14	0.7	83
133	Pakistani chicken curry	531	268	27	25	98	1.3	0.12	0.6	809
134	Bengali chicken curry	460	316	34	29	157	1.8	0.18	0.9	677
135	Bengali chicken bhuna	384	411	34	36	201	1.8	0.21	1.2	549
136	Ismaili chicken/potato curry	341	276	14	21	108	0.9	0.12	0.6	518
137	Bengali chicken/potato curry	210	294	20	24	128	0.9	0.14	0.7	306
138	Pakistani roast chicken	343	387	18	32	234	0.9	0.22	1.3	477
139	Punjabi matar paneer	N	N	437	N	314	1.8	N	N	N
140	Punjabi matar paneer/potato	N	N	76	N	71	0.6	N	N	N
141	Punjabi palak paneer	N	N	290	N	166	1.9	N	N	N
142	Bengali egg curry	543	288	83	26	180	2.7	0.12	1.2	803

Meat dishes 131-138   Egg and cheese dishes 139-142

Vitamin content per 100g

No	Recipe	REQ ug	Vit. D ug	Vit. E mg	Vit. B$_1$ mg	Vit. B$_2$ mg	Niacin mg	Vit.B6 mg	Vit. B$_{12}$ ug	Folate ug	Vit. C mg
131	Punjabi chicken curry	4	Tr	0.59	0.04	0.07	3.8	0.16	Tr	6	1
132	Punjabi chicken curry with yogurt	23	Tr	0.34	0.04	0.08	3.7	0.16	Tr	6	2
133	Pakistani chicken curry	12	Tr	2.18	0.03	0.05	2.4	0.12	Tr	5	3
134	Bengali chicken curry	2	Tr	0.11	0.04	0.08	4.3	0.18	Tr	6	2
135	Bengali chicken bhuna	52	Tr	2.43	0.05	0.12	5.5	0.22	Tr	7	1
136	Ismaili chicken/potato curry	13	Tr	0.59	0.04	0.06	2.9	0.16	Tr	7	3
137	Bengali chicken/potato curry	8	Tr	1.05	0.05	0.07	3.5	0.17	Tr	7	1
138	Pakistani roast chicken	23	Tr	0.10	0.05	0.13	6.7	0.24	Tr	7	Tr
139	Punjabi matar paneer	N	0.2	N	N	N	N	N	N	N	5
140	Punjabi matar paneer/potato	N	0.3	N	N	N	N	N	N	N	4
141	Punjabi palek paneer	N	Tr	N	N	N	N	N	N	N	8
142	Bengali egg curry	177	1.3	3.68	0.17	0.37	3.7	0.22	1.9	24	2

Fish Dishes

Fish dishes 143 - 158

Composition of food per 100g

No	Recipe	Main Ingredients	Water g	Protein g	Fat g	CHO g	Energy kcals	Energy kj
143	Ismaili masala fish	new potatoes, coley, tomatoes, veg. oil	67.1	8.7	8.4	11.3	150	627
144	Bengali baim fish and potato	gojar (baim) fish, old potatoes, onions, veg. oil	64.9	15.3	7.4	6.3	144	600
145	Bengali boal fish curry	boal fish, onions, corn oil	71.9	8.9	8.8	2.0	120	500
146	Bengali gargot (ayr) curry	ayr fish, onions, veg. oil	79.5	7.8	7.7	0.7	101	419
147	Bengali gojar shutki curry	onions, dry gojar fish, veg. oil	42.1	19.0	24.3	4.3	300	1241
148	Bengali hidol fish chutney	onions, dry hidol fish, veg. oil	62.8	7.3	14.6	6.2	168	698
149	Bengali illish fish curry	hilsa (illish) fish, onions, veg. oil	58.3	14.0	20.4	1.5	243	1005
150	Bengali ketchki fish curry	ketchki fish, onions, veg. oil	68.3	11.1	8.7	4.9	134	557
151	Bengali koi fish curry	koi fish, onions, sunfl. oil	67.9	7.2	15.8	4.1	181	750
152	Bengali magur fish curry	magur fish, onions, sunfl. oil	76.5	10.3	8.8	3.0	129	534
153	Bengali pabda fish curry	pabda fish, onions, sunfl. oil	76.4	11.2	5.1	4.3	106	441
154	Bengali prawn bhuna	prawns, tomatoes, onions, veg. oil	63.7	15.9	11.1	3.8	178	742
155	Bengali rui fish curry	rohu (rui) fish, onions, corn oil	73.7	9.0	9.8	1.7	126	522
156	Bengali rui fish and potato curry	rohu, old potatoes, onions, corn oil	74.6	8.3	7.1	5.7	118	490
157	Bengali sardines curry	sardines, onions, veg. oil	81.5	7.0	7.7	1.1	98	408
158	Bengali tengra fish curry	tengra, corn oil, garlic, coriander	71	11.7	11.9	2.5	163	675

Fish dishes 143 - 158

Composition of food per 100g

No	Recipe	PUFA g	MUFA g	SFA g	Chol mg	Starch g	Sugar g	NSP g
143	Ismaili masala fish	3.7	3.0	0.9	17	7.9	3.0	1.2
144	Bengali baim fish and potato	N	N	N	N	4.1	0.8	0.6
145	Bengali boal fish curry	N	N	N	N	0.1	1.4	0.4
146	Bengali gargot (ayr) curry	N	N	N	0	0.0	0.5	0.1
147	Bengali gojar shutki curry	N	N	N	N	0.0	1.9	0.7
148	Bengali hidol fish chutney	N	N	N	N	0.0	4.4	1.1
149	Bengali illish fish curry	N	N	N	N	0.0	1.0	0.4
150	Bengali ketcnki fish curry	N	N	N	N	0.2	1.8	1.9
151	Bengali koi fish curry	N	N	N	N	0.1	1.1	0.3
152	Bengali maçur fish curry	N	N	N	N	0.1	0.6	0.2
153	Bengali pabda fish curry	N	N	N	N	0.1	1.2	0.4
154	Bengali prawn bhuna	5.1	3.8	1.2	160	0.1	2.7	1.1
155	Bengali rui f sh curry	N	N	N	N	0.0	1.1	0.3
156	Bengali rui f sh and potato curry	N	N	N	N	4.7	0.7	0.5
157	Bengali sarcines curry	3.0	2.4	1.3	4	0.2	0.7	0.2
158	Bengali tençra fish curry	N	N	N	N	0.1	0.7	0.2

Fish dishes 143 - 158

Inorganic constituents per 100g

No	Recipe	Na mg	K mg	Ca mg	Mg mg	P mg	Fe mg	Cu mg	Zn mg	Cl mg
143	Ismaili masala fish	412	508	25	30	172	1.0	0.12	0.5	599
144	Bengali baim fish and potato	1859	N	151	N	18	1.2	N	N	N
145	Bengali boal fish curry	N	N	59	11	280	1.1	0.06	0.5	N
146	Bengali gargot (ayr) curry	N	N	187	N	91	0.7	N	N	N
147	Bengali gojar shutki curry	3037	N	202	N	19	2.1	N	N	N
148	Bengali hidol fish chutney	1283	N	538	N	34	5.4	N	N	N
149	Bengali illish fish curry	593	174	128	N	186	2.0	N	N	N
150	Bengali ketchki fish curry	537	N	432	N	35	5.3	N	N	N
151	Bengali koi fish curry	466	N	206	N	24	1.7	N	N	N
152	Bengali magur fish curry	357	N	324	N	14	1.1	N	N	N
153	Bengali pabda fish curry	547	N	187	N	11	1.3	N	N	N
154	Bengali prawn bhuna	1053	297	98	42	140	2.3	0.16	1.1	1542
155	Bengali rui fish curry	400	236	N	16	107	1.2	0.10	N	N
156	Bengali rui fish and potato curry	350	272	N	15	97	0.7	0.09	N	N
157	Bengali sardines curry	172	15	36	15	97	0.9	0.06	0.4	249
158	Bengali tengra fish curry	242	63	170	7	9.4	1.6	0.02	0.6	373

Fish dishes 143 - 158

No	Recipe	REQ ug	Vit. D ug	Vit. E mg	Vit. B1 mg	Vit. B2 mg	Niacin mg	Vit.B6 mg	Vit. B12 ug	Folate ug	Vit. C mg
143	Ismaili masala fish	47	0.0	0.67	0.16	0.11	3.2	0.41	1.2	11	8
144	Bengali baim fish and potato	10	N	N	N	N	N	N	N	5	2
145	Bengali boal fish curry	16	N	N	N	N	3.1	N	N	N	N
146	Bengali garçot (ayr) curry	30	Tr	N	N	N	1.7	N	N	N	1
147	Bengali gojar shutki curry	36	N	N	N	N	N	N	N	N	N
148	Benali hidol fish chutney	129	N	N	N	N	N	N	N	N	2
149	Bengali illish fish curry	14	N	N	N	N	N	N	N	N	2
150	Bengali ketchki fish curry	59	N	N	N	N	N	N	N	N	2
151	Bengali koi fish curry	90	N	N	N	N	N	N	N	N	8
152	Bengali maçur fish curry	58	N	N	N	N	N	N	N	N	1
153	Bengali pabda fish curry	19	N	N	N	N	N	N	N	N	1
154	Bengali prawn bhuna	49	N	N	0.08	0.12	1.2	0.16	5.7	N	7
155	Bengali rui fish curry	47	N	N	0.05	0.05	2.1	N	2.5	N	1
156	Bengali rui fish and potato curry	23	N	N	N	0.04	2.0	N	2.2	N	2
157	Bengali sardines curry	58	3.5	0.13	0.02	0.09	3.3	0.15	3.5	2	Tr
158	Bengali tengra fish curry	39	N	N	N	N	N	N	N	N	1

Sweet Dishes

Sweet dishes 159 - 164

Composition of food per 100g

No	Recipe	Main Ingredients	Water g	Protein g	Fat g	CHO g	Energy kcals	Energy kj
159	Punjabi oat porridge (dhuri)	milk, oatmeal, sugar, ghee, almonds	79.3	2.6	4.4	14.0	102	431
160	Pakistani kheer	milk, white rice, sugar	65.3	2.9	3.0	29.4	151	637
161	Pakistani sevia	sugar, vermicelli, veg. ghee, almonds, coconut	54.6	3.7	10.8	30.0	226	945
162	Pakistani zarda	basmati rice, sugar sunfl oil, almonds	29.0	4.5	9.9	56.0	330	1379
163	Ismaili thepla	white flour, sunfl. oil, sugar, eggs, semi-skim milk	11.6	5.9	26.6	57.4	477	1997
164	Bengali sandesh sweet	white flour, corn oil, sugar	41.3	3.9	16.2	40.0	311	1304

No	Recipe	PUFA g	MUFA g	SFA g	Chol mg	Starch g	Sugar g	NSP g
159	Punjabi oat porridge (dhuri)	0.2	1.0	1.9	9	9.0	5.1	0.9
160	Pakistani kheer	0.1	0.9	1.9	11	5.0	24.4	0.0
161	Pakistani sevia	N	N	N	9	7.6	22.4	0.9
162	Pakistani zarda	5.6	2.5	1.1	0	42.8	13.2	0.4
163	Ismaili thepla	16.0	5.5	3.5	35	35.4	22.0	1.4
164	Bengali sandesh sweet	9.3	3.9	2.1	0	31.8	8.3	1.3

Sweet dishes 159 - 164

Inorganic constituents per 100g

No	Recipe	Na mg	K mg	Ca mg	Mg mg	P mg	Fe mg	Cu mg	Zn mg	Cl mg
159	Punjabi oat porridge (dhuri)	19	90	40	19	76	0.6	0.04	0.6	361
160	Pakistani kheer	43	115	90	9	76	0.1	0.02	0.4	77
161	Pakistani sevia	36	150	82	24	89	1.1	0.10	0.6	71
162	Pakistani zarda	4	79	16	13	52	1.0	0.12	0.8	15
163	Ismaili thepla	20	102	84	13	80	1.4	0.09	0.5	62
164	Bengali sandesh sweet	1	63	58	8	46	0.8	0.06	0.3	34

No	Recipe	REQ ug	Vit. D ug	Vit. E mg	Vit. B1 mg	Vit. B2 mg	Niacin mg	Vit. B6 mg	Vit. B12 ug	Folate ug	Vit. C mg
159	Punjabi oat porridge (dhuri)	29	0.1	0.51	0.04	0.04	0.4	0.02	0.1	5	0
160	Pakistani kheer	43	Tr	0.08	0.04	0.12	0.7	0.05	0.3	5	Tr
161	Pakistani sevia	34	Tr	1.38	0.05	0.13	1.0	0.05	0.2	6	Tr
162	Pakistani zarda	0	0	4.70	0.03	0.02	0.1	0.10	0	6	0
163	Ismaili thepla	19	0.2	12.44	0.10	0.05	1.3	0.05	0.3	8	Tr
164	Bengali sandesh sweet	0	0	2.82	0.08	0.01	0.9	0.04	0	5	0

SECTION 2

Energy and nutrient composition of purchased cooked dishes by direct laboratory analysis

Composition of food per 100g

No	Recipe	Main Ingredients	Water g	Protein g	Fat g	CHO g	Energy kcals	Energy kj
165	Bengali meat samosa	fried pastry, meat and veg. filling	39.8	11.1	16.9	19.2	320	1340
166	Ismaili meat samosa	fried pastry, meat and veg. filling	46.0	15.2	11.4	23.6	260	1085
167	Pakistani meat samosa	fried pastry, meat and veg. filling	48.5	10.0	13.3	20.7	255	1065
168	Bengali vegetable samosa	fried pastry, peas and veg. filling	34.9	4.5	25.6	30.5	378	1580
169	Pakistani vegetable samosa	fried pastry, peas and veg. filling	38.1	4.4	20.2	34.2	334	1395
170	Bengali kebab	minced lamb, shaped and grilled	57.3	21.8	12.2	1.5	204	850
171	Ismaili kebab	minced lamb, shaped and grilled	47.0	16.6	9.4	15.1	260	1085
172	Ismaili bhajia	fried potato/onion in chick pea batter	46.7	8.8	14.0	20.6	269	1125
173	Ismaili ganthia	fried gram flour spicy snack	2.9	16.5	36.2	29.3	542	2265
174	Ismaili paratha	fried thick chapati with added fat	24.4	6.1	19.1	48.8	373	1560
175	Pakistani biryani	meat, rice, potatoes, yogurt oil/ghee	56.3	9.0	7.1	29.3	199	830
176	Pakistani mithai	mixture of traditional sweetmeats	15.2	10.0	19.3	49.4	415	1735

Nutrient composition of purchased cooked dishes by direct laboratory analysis

Composition of food per 100g

No	Food	PUFA g	MUFA g	SFA g	NSP g	Na mg	K mg	Ca mg	Fe mg	Zn mg	Folate ug	Vit. C mg
165	Bengali meat samosa	2.2	8.4	4.2	1.9	409	223	24	1.4	2.0	10	1
166	Ismaili meat samosa	2.4	6.6	3.1	1.5	799	275	50	1.9	2.2	22	Tr
167	Pakistani meat samosa	2.4	6.0	3.0	2.0	597	191	67	1.2	1.9	13	1
168	Bengali vegetable samosa	N	N	N	1.2	319	244	58	0.8	1.1	N	Tr
169	Pakistani vegetable samosa	1.7	11.2	5.0	1.8	384	248	56	0.9	0.9	11	Tr
170	Bengali kebab	4.2	4.8	1.3	1.0	1038	593	38	2.3	2.8	10	Tr
171	Ismaili kebab	2.2	2.4	0.9	1.9	546	382	31	2.1	2.0	4	Tr
172	Ismaili bhajia	1.5	7.0	4.3	2.9	570	432	31	1.8	1.1	9	Tr
173	Ismaili ganthia	N	N	N	4.2	N	N	61	2.6	2.1	N	Tr
174	Ismaili paratha	N	N	N	2.4	170	132	188	1.3	1.6	N	Tr
175	Pakistani biryani	1.3	3.2	1.5	0.6	149	304	29	1.0	1.4	11	Tr
176	Pakistani mithai	N	N	N	0.8	242	441	237	0.6	1.4	2	1

Energy and nutrient content of some raw Bangladeshi fish by direct laboratory analysis

Composition of food per 100g

No	Food	Description	Water g	Protein g	Fat g	CHO g	Energy kcals	Energy kj
177	Kanla - fresh	white fish, very bony, length 7cm	72.4	19.7	2.6	3.1	117	490
178	Ketchki - fresh	white fish, eaten whole, length 2-3cm	83.6	12.5	1.8	0.7	65	270
179	Baim - fresh	eel fish, oily, length 30-40cm	74.8	18.0	4.4	1.4	116	485
180	Baim shutki - dry	dried eel fish, oily	9.1	63.1	15.8	0.6	337	1410
181	Shoal - fresh	white fish, length 40-60cm	75.8	18.8	3.4	0.9	109	455
182	Shoal shutki - dry	dried shoal	9.7	71.4	9.5	0.4	302	1260
183	Gojar	white fish similar to shoal but larger	25.7	55.9	0.8	3.9	222	930
184	Hidol shutki - dry	oily fish, flat, length 5-7cm, pungent	42.6	26.1	20.4	0.2	256	1070

Nutrient content of some raw Bangladeshi fish by direct laboratory analysis

Composition of food per 100g

No	Food	PUFA g	MUFA g	SFA g	NSP g	Na g	K g	Ca mg	Fe g	Zn g	Folate g	Vit. C g
177	Kanla - fresh	N	N	N	0	162	140	403	1.3	N	N	0
178	Ketchki - fresh	N	N	N	0	48	85	482	1.4	N	N	0
179	Baim - fresh	N	N	N	0	138	243	168	1.3	N	N	0
180	Baim shutki - dry	N	N	N	0	581	742	1612	9.3	N	N	0
181	Shoal - fresh	N	N	N	0	124	239	93	0.7	N	N	0
182	Shoal shutki - dry	N	N	N	0	628	1107	1098	8.7	N	N	0
183	Gojar	N	N	N	0	4917	1708	545	2.9	N	N	0
184	Hidol shutki - dry	N	N	N	0	267	393	2225	20.3	N	N	0

RECIPES FOR COMMONLY-CONSUMED TRADITIONAL DISHES IN SECTION 1

In each case the recipe nearest the mean for all samples is given. The numbers correspond to the dishes in Section 1 of the food composition tables.

Where available the ingredients and energy and proximate nutrient contents of a similar recipe where the fat content was appreciably lower is given.

Vegetable Dishes

Vegetable dishes

1. PUNJABI MIXED VEGETABLE CURRY

Average

360g	carrots
350g	potatoes
315g	onions
300g	peas
160g	tinned tomatoes
125g	corn oil
9g	ginger
7g	garlic

(salt, whole cumin, green/red chilli, garam masala and coriander leaves to garnish)

Cooked Weight 1330g

Lower fat

348g	carrots
214g	potatoes
164g	peas
108g	fresh tomatoes
90g	onions
20g	sunflower oil

(Salt, garlic, ginger, spices as above)

Cooked Weight 795g

Heat oil, add spices and fry. Add prepared vegetables cut to size and stir. Add tomatoes, then remaining ingredients and extra water if necessary. Cook to desired consistency.

Nutrient content per 100g cooked weight

	Water	Protein	Fat	CHO	NSP	Energy	Energy
	g	g	g	g	g	kcals	kj
Average	74	2.5	9.8	11.2	2.6	140	580
Lower fat	78	2.6	3.2	12.4	2.8	85	360

2. GUJARATI MIXED VEGETABLE CURRY

Average

1180g	peas
350g	aubergine
225g	tomatoes
75g	corn oil
	water

(Salt, whole cumin and fenugreek, turmeric, cumin, chilli powder, chopped coriander)

Cooked weight 2070g

Heat oil, add cumin and fenugreek. When it starts to splutter add spices and peeled vegetables cut to desired size and stir. Add tomatoes and stir. Add remaining ingredients and stir. Add water if necessary. Cook on medium heat until vegetables are cooked and the sauce is of desired consistency. Garnish with chopped coriander when serving.

Nutrient content per 100g cooked weight

	Water	Protein	Fat	CHO	NSP	Energy	Energy
	g	g	g	g	g	kcals	kj
Average	82	3.6	4.4	6.3	3.5	78	325

Vegetable dishes

3. ISMAILI MIXED VEGETABLE CURRY

Average

400g	potatoes
224g	frozen mixed veg.
108g	onions
108g	tinned tomatoes
24g	tomato puree
5g	green chillies

32g	sunflower oil
1g	cumin powder
1g	coriander powder
1g	turmeric powder
5g	fresh coriander

Cooked Weight 830g

Boil potatoes and mixed vegetables. Fry onions and spices. Add vegetables and potatoes with some water originally used to boil vegetables. Garnish with coriander.

Nutrient content per 100g cooked weight

	Water	Protein	Fat	CHO	NSP	Energy	Energy
	g	g	g	g	g	kcals	kj
Average	79	2.2	4.2	11.4	1.6	90	375

4. PAKISTANI MIXED VEGETABLE CURRY

Average

400g	frozen mixed vegetables
80g	onions
10g	garlic
10g	ginger
8g	tomatoes
6g	fresh coriander

6g	salt
6g	sunflower oil
4g	chilli powder
4g	green chillies
2g	garam masala

Cooked Weight 538g

Fry onions and spices. Add tomatoes, vegetables and water. Simmer till done. Garnish with green chillies and coriander.

Nutrient content per 100g cooked weight

	Water	Protein	Fat	CHO	NSP	Energy	Energy
	g	g	g	g	g	kcals	kj
Average	84	2.8	1.5	7.5	2.5	50	215

Vegetable dishes

5. BENGALI MIXED VEGETABLE BHAJI

Average

256g	mixed veg. (frozen)	64g	vegetable oil
116g	onions	6g	green chillies
114g	potatoes	2g	salt

Cooked Weight 334g

Boil vegetables. Fry onions, potatoes and spices. Add the boiled vegetables.

Lower Fat

514g	mixed veg. (frozen)	12g	salt
96g	onions	6g	green chillies
50g	corn oil	2g	turmeric

Cooked Weight 530g

Fry onions, chillies with spices. Add frozen vegetables and cook till done.

Nutrient content per 100g cooked weight

	Water	Protein	Fat	CHO	NSP	Energy	Energy
	g	g	g	g	g	kcals	kj
Average	64	2.5	19.7	11.2	3.0	230	950
Lower fat	72	3.5	10.0	7.8	2.4	130	550

6. PUNJABI SAAG (SPINACH) CURRY

Average

2310g	spinach	50g	ghee
125g	onions	15g	ginger
120g	corn flour	10g	garlic
50g	chilli (green)		

Cooked Weight 2910g

Trim and wash the greens, chop coarsely, put in large pot and add a little water, cook till tender. Blend ginger, garlic and chilli. Remove greens from pan with slotted spoon and add to blender. Blend to a smooth paste. Heat ghee in a large pot over medium flame, add cornflour and cook without browning. Put in pureed greens and some salt. Cook for about 10mins.

Nutrient content per 100g cooked weight

	Water	Protein	Fat	CHO	NSP	Energy	Energy
	g	g	g	g	g	kcals	kj
Average	86	2.4	2.4	5.7	1.8	55	225

Vegetable dishes

7. GUJARATI SPINACH CURRY

Average

775g	spinach
375g	tomatoes
100g	oil

(salt, mustard seeds, turmeric, ground cumin/coriander, chilli powder, garlic, coriander leaves to garnish)

Cooked Weigh: 750g

Wash and chcp spinach. Heat oil, add mustard seeds then add tomatoes and remaining ingredients, fry for 5-7 minutes. Add spinach and cook till the greens are tender.

Nutrient content per 100g cooked weight

	Water g	Protein g	Fat g	CHO g	NSP g	Energy kcals	Energy kj
Average	74	2.9	14.2	7.0	2.4	150	625

8. PAKISTANI SPINACH CURRY (PALAK)

Average

1864g	spinach
192g	butter ghee
142g	onions
74g	green chillies
66g	chick pea flour
26g	ginger
26g	salt

Cooked Weight 2295g

Boil spinach. Add chillies and salt. Cook in pressure cooker. Mash cooked spinach and mix in gram flour. Add boiling water and heat. Separately melt ghee and fry onions and ginger till brown. Add spinach and stir.

Nutrient content per 100g cooked weight

	Water g	Protein g	Fat g	CHO g	NSP g	Energy kcals	Energy kj
Average	78	3.0	9.2	3.7	2.2	110	450

Vegetable dishes

9. BENGALI SPINACH BHAJI

Average

538g	fresh spinach	12g	salt
26g	onions	10g	fresh garlic
22g	sunflower oil	8g	green chillies
14g	fresh coriander		

Cooked weight 246g

Boil spinach. Fry onions and garlic. Add spices and boiled drained spinach.

Lower Fat

498g	fresh spinach	14g	green chillies
102g	onions	6g	salt
44g	corn oil	2g	turmeric
18g	garlic		

Cooked Weight 504g

Fry onions. Add spices and spinach and cook till done.

Nutrient content per 100g cooked weight

	Water g	Protein g	Fat g	CHO g	NSP g	Energy kcals	Energy kj
Average	60	6.8	10.8	5.1	4.9	145	595
Lower fat	85	3.4	5.8	3.8	2.5	80	335

10. GUJARATI SPINACH (METHI) BHAJI

Average

890g	spinach	(salt, mustard seeds, turmeric,
120g	tomatoes	ground cumin/coriander
100g	onions	chilli powder, garlic, coriander leaves
35g	corn oil	to garnish)
60g	fenugreek	

Cooked Weight 760g

Wash and chop spinach and fenugreek. Heat oil, add mustard seeds. Fry chopped onions with garlic pieces until lightly brown. Add tomatoes and remaining ingredients, fry for 5-7 minutes. Add spinach and fenugreek and mix well. Cook till the greens are tender.

Nutrient content per 100g cooked weight

	Water g	Protein g	Fat g	CHO g	NSP g	Energy kcals	Energy kj
Average	73	5.8	6.5	7.8	3.5	110	420

Vegetable dishes

11. PUNJABI SPINACH AND POTATO CURRY

Average

430g	spinach	10g	chilli
254g	potatoes	10g	garlic
40g	sunflower oil	(salt)	

Cooked Weight 530g

Cook spinach in boiling water, drain and press out excess water. Fry chopped onions and garlic. Mix well, add peeled and chopped potatoes and chilli. Add spinach, salt and some water. Cook until potatoes are tender.

Nutrient content per 100g cooked weight

	Water	Protein	Fat	CHO	NSP	Energy	Energy
	g	g	g	g	g	kcals	kj
Average	74	3.5	8.3	10.1	2.5	125	530

12. PUNJABI AUBERGINE CURRY

Average

2435g	aubergines	94g	tomatoes
326g	onions	19g	ginger
129g	ghee	16g	chillies
(salt)			

Cooked Weight 2119g

Lower Fat

750g	aubergines	50g	fried onions
397g	tinned tomatoes	17g	chillies
(salt)			

Cooked Weight 1000g

Slice aubergines and salt for 30-40 minutes. Fry aubergines until coloured and drain in colander. Put fried aubergine, chopped onions, and remaining ingredients in a pan with water and simmer till done (Lower fat version, omit frying stage).

Nutrient content per 100g cooked weight

	Water	Protein	Fat	CHO	NSP	Energy	Energy
		g	g	g	g	kcals	kj
Average	72	2.4	8.1	14.2	2.7	135	565
Lower fat	92	1.3	0.9	3.7	2.0	30	115

13. GUJARATI AUBERGINE BHAJI

Average

310g aubergines
25g   corn oil
5g   turmeric

(salt, mustard seeds, coriander/cumin
powder, garlic, chilli)

Cooked Weight 440g

Cut aubergines into cubes. Heat oil and add mustard seeds and garlic pieces. Add spices and fry for a few minutes. Add remaining aubergines and a small amount of water and cook till aubergines are done and curry is quite dry.

Nutrient content per 100g cooked weight

	Water	Protein	Fat	CHO	NSP	Energy	Energy
	g	g	g	g	g	kcals	kj
Average	86	0.8	7.7	2.0	1.8	80	330

14. GUJARATI AUBERGINE AND TOMATOES CURRY

Average

550g aubergines
210g tomatoes
90g   groundnut oil

(salt, mustard seeds, coriander/
cumin powder, turmeric, garlic, chilli)

Cooked Weight 760g

Lower Fat

290g aubergines
160g tomatoes
30g   vegetable oil
(salt, spices as above)

Cooked Weight 440g

Heat oil and add mustard seeds and garlic pieces. Add tomatoes and spices and fry for a few minutes. Add remaining aubergines, a small amount of water and cook till quite dry.

Nutrient content per 100g cooked weight

	Water	Protein	Fat	CHO	NSP	Energy	Energy
	g	g	g	g	g	kcals	kj
Average	81	0.9	12.2	2.4	1.6	120	500
Lower fat	89	0.8	6.0	2.3	1.6	65	270

15. PUNJABI AUBERGINE AND POTATO CURRY

Average

512g	aubergines	216g	tomatoes
440g	onions	86g	oil
350g	potatoes	5g	chilli powder

(salt, whole cumin, turmeric, garam masala)

Cooked Weight 1360g

Lower fat

620g	onions	210g	tomatoes
590g	aubergines	80g	corn oil
454g	potatoes	16g	chillies

(salt and spices as above)

Cooked Weight 1050g

Heat oil, fry onions, add spices and fry. Add prepared vegetables cut to size and stir. Add tomatoes, then remaining ingredients and extra water if necessary. Cook to desired consistency.

Nutrient content per 100g cooked weight

	Water	Protein	Fat	CHO	NSP	Energy	Energy
	g	g	g	g	g	kcals	kj
Average	81	1.5	6.7	8.3	1.7	95	400
Lower fat	78	2.0	3.7	12.0	2.3	85	360

16. GUJARATI POTATO CURRY

Average

1510g	potatoes
80g	corn oil

(salt, whole cumin seeds, ground coriander/cumin, turmeric and chilli, coriander leaves to garnish)

Cooked Weight 1400g

Lower Fat

730g	potatoes
50g	corn oil

Cooked Weight 1060g

Peel and wash potatoes and cut into cubes. Heat oil and add cumin. When it starts to splutter add spices and stir. Add potatoes and some water and cook on a low heat till they are done. Coriander to garnish.

Nutrient content per 100g cooked weight

	Water	Protein	Fat	CHO	NSP	Energy	Energy
	g	g	g	g	g	kcals	kj
Average	72	2.3	5.9	18.5	1.4	132	555
Lower fat	81	1.5	4.9	11.9	0.9	95	400

Vegetable dishes

17. PAKISTANI POTATO CURRY

Average

225g	chopped potatoes
120g	tinned tomatoes
65g	chopped onions
50g	corn oil
15g	ginger
8g	coriander

6g	garlic
4g	salt
3g	coriander
3g	fresh green chillies
2g	cumin
2g	turmeric

Cooked Weight 603g

Lower Fat

512g	potatoes
198g	tinned tomatoes
98g	onions
60g	corn oil
10g	fresh coriander
8g	ginger
6g	garlic

6g	salt
3g	coriander powder
2g	black pepper
2g	cumin
2g	green chillies
2g	turmeric

Cooked Weight 1156g

Fry onions and spices. Add tomatoes, potatoes and water. Cook till done. Garnish with coriander.

Nutrient content per 100g cooked weight

	Water g	Protein g	Fat g	CHO g	NSP g	Energy kcals	Energy kj
Average	80	1.3	8.5	7.8	0.7	110	450
Lower fat	82	1.4	5.3	9.1	0.9	87	364

18. BENGALI POTATO BHAJI

Average

1026g	potatoes
154g	onions
55g	vegetable oil
80g	capsicums

16g	salt
2g	green chillies
2g	turmeric
2g	fenugreek seeds

Cooked Weight 1022g

Fry onions and spices until brown. Add chillies and capsicums. Cut potatoes into small cubes and fry with the above till cooked.

Lower Fat

750g	potatoes
150g	onions
30g	mix vegetable oil
36g	fresh coriander

15g	salt
10g	green chillies
2g	turmeric

Cooked Weight 824g

Fry onions and spices. Add cubed potatoes, chillies and coriander. Cover and cook till done.

Nutrient content per 100g cooked weight

	Water g	Protein g	Fat g	CHO g	NSP g	Energy kcals	Energy kj
Average	69	2.4	5.7	18.7	1.6	130	545
Lower fat	72	2.3	3.9	17.2	1.4	110	460

Vegetable dishes

19. PUNJABI POTATO, ONION, TOMATO CURRY

Average

492g	potatoes	112g	onions
208g	tinned tomatoes	100g	sunflower oil

(salt, whole cumin, turmeric, garlic, ginger, green chilli, garam masala)

Cooked Weight 1700g

Lower Fat

860g	potatoes	15g	ginger
360g	onions	14g	coriander
195g	tomatoes	13g	chillies
50g	butter	9g	garlic

(salt, whole cumin, turmeric)

Cooked Weight 1210g

Heat oil, fry onions, add spices and fry. Add prepared vegetables cut to size and stir. Add tomatoes, then remaining ingredients and extra water if necessary. Cook to desired consistency.

Nutrient content per 100g cooked weight

	Water	Protein	Fat	CHO	NSP	Energy	Energy
	g	g	g	g	g	kcals	kj
Average	87	0.8	6.0	5.9	0.6	80	330
Lower fat	80	1.4	3.0	13.2	1.1	80	330

20. PUNJABI POTATO AND GREEN PEPPER CURRY

Average

1320g	potatoes	90g	onions
305g	green peppers	30g	green chilli
235g	tinned tomatoes	15g	garlic
145g	corn oil		

(salt, whole cumin, turmeric, garam masala)

Cooked Weight 1640g

Lower Fat

574g	green peppers	84g	coriander leaves
392g	onions	37g	corn oil
248g	potatoes	35g	tomato puree

(salt, whole cumin, turmeric, garlic, ginger, green chilli, garam masala)

Cooked Weight 996g

Heat oil, fry spices, add onions and fry. Add prepared vegetables cut to size and stir. Add tomatoes (or tomato paste), then remaining ingredients and extra water if necessary. Cook to desired consistency.

Nutrient content per 100g cooked weight

	Water	Protein	Fat	CHO	NSP	Energy	Energy
	g	g	g	g	g	kcals	kj
Average	71	2.2	9.1	15.5	1.6	150	620
Lower fat	82	1.8	4.0	9.5	1.9	80	330

Vegetable dishes

21. GUJARATI POTATO AND TOMATO CURRY

Average

810g	potatoes	(salt, whole cumin, ground turmeric,
180g	tomatoes	cumin, coriander and chilli chopped
135g	vegetable oil	coriander garnish)

Cooked Weight 1530g

Lower Fat

980g	potatoes	(salt and spices as above)
235g	tomatoes	
115g	vegetable oil	

Cooked Weight 1700g

Peel and wash potatoes and cut into cubes. Heat oil and add cumin. When it starts to splutter add spices and stir, then add tomatoes and potatoes and cook on a low heat till potatoes are cooked. May need a little water. Garnish with chopped coriander.

Nutrient content per 100g cooked weight

	Water	Protein	Fat	CHO	NSP	Energy	Energy
		g	g	g	g	kcals	kj
Average	79	1.2	8.9	9.5	0.8	120	500
Lower fat	82	1.3	5.7	10.0	0.9	95	400

22. PAKISTANI ALOO PAKORA

350g	Chick pea flour	6g	salt
200g	old potatoes	5g	chilli powder
100g	sunflower oil	4g	chilli
50g	onions	3g	coriander leaves - dried
20g	spinach	3g	cumin seeds

Cooked Weight 750g

Thinly slice the potatoes. Mix all the ingredients except the oil with sufficient water to form a thick batter. Spoon the mixture into the hot oil and fry till golden brown.

Nutrient content per 100g cooked weight

	Water	Protein	Fat	CHO	NSP	Energy	Energy
		g	g	g	g	kcals	kj
Average	35	10.3	16.3	28.8	5.6	295	1230

Vegetable dishes

23. PUNJABI POTATO AND COURGETTE CURRY

Average

562g	potatoes	80g	sunflower oil
434g	courgettes	20g	garlic
144g	tomato puree	3g	chillies
114g	onions		

(salt, whole cumin, turmeric, ginger, garam masala)

Cooked Weight 1167g

Lower Fat

660g	courgettes	55g	soya oil
370g	potatoes	50g	ginger
350g	tomatoes	15g	garlic
325g	onions	10g	chillies

(salt, whole cumin, turmeric)

Cooked Weight 1560g

Heat oil, fry spices, add onions and fry. Add prepared vegetables cut to size and stir. Add tomatoes (or tomato paste), then remaining ingredients and extra water if necessary. Cook to desired consistency.

Nutrient content per 100g cooked weight

	Water	Protein	Fat	CHO	NSP	Energy	Energy
	g	g	g	g	g	kcals	kj
Average	75	2.5	7.2	1.6	1.5	120	490
Lower fat	75	1.9	3.8	7.7	1.2	70	295

24. PUNJABI BHINDI (OKRA)

Average

420g	okra	90g	corn oil
210g	onions	15g	garlic
145g	tinned tomatoes	15g	ginger

(salt, ground cumin, lemon juice)

Cooked Weight 890g

Lower fat

430g	okra	60g	corn oil
350g	onions	6g	cumin
130g	tomatoes		

(salt, lemon juice)

Cooked Weight 1295g

Fry garlic and finely sliced onions in oil. Put in okra stir and fry. Add tomatoes and remaining ingredients and cook till tender.

Nutrient content per 100g cooked weight

	Water	Protein	Fat	CHO	NSP	Energy	Energy
	g	g	g	g	g	kcals	kj
Average	79	1.9	10.7	4.2	2.4	120	490
Lower fat	89	1.3	4.8	3.3	1.7	60	245

Vegetable dishes

25. GUJARATI BHINDA (OKRA)

Average

510g bhinda
135g vegetable oil
(salt, ajma seeds, ground turmeric, coriander, cumin and chilli)

Cooked Weight 440g

Lower Fat

300g bhinda
100g onions
70g cotton seed oil

Cooked Weight 420g

Wipe okra with a damp cloth. Top and tail and cut lengthwise into 2. Heat oil and add ajma, add onions and fry till soft. Add okra and stir fry on low-medium heat for half hour. Add spices and stir gently till the oil starts to ooze out and the texture looks like dry pickle.

Nutrient content per 100g cooked weight

	Water	Protein	Fat	CHO	NSP	Energy	Energy
		g	g	g	g	kcals	kj
Average	54	3.3	31.8	3.5	4.6	310	1285
Lower fat	71	2.3	17.3	4.0	3.2	180	740

26. GUJARATI BHINDI AND TOMATOES

Average

200g bhindi
205g canned tomatoes
15g corn oil
(salt and spices as recipe no 25)

Cooked Weight 350g

Wipe okra with a damp cloth. Top and tail and cut lengthwise into 2. Heat oil and add ajma, add tomatoes. Add okra and stir fry on low-medium heat for half hour. Add spices and stir gently till the oil starts to ooze out and the texture looks like dry pickle.

Nutrient content per 100g cooked weight

	Water	Protein	Fat	CHO	NSP	Energy	Energy
		g	g	g	g	kcals	kj
Average	85	2.2	4.9	3.5	2.7	65	275

Vegetable dishes

27. PAKISTANI BHINDI (OKRA)

Average

228g	okra	4g	ground coriander
200g	onions	4g	salt
110g	fresh tomatoes	2g	chilli powder
38g	sunflower oil	1g	turmeric

Cooked Weight 584g

Brown onions in oil. Add tomatoes and spices. Add okra and stir fry. Cover and simmer till done.

Nutrient content per 100g cooked weight

	Water	Protein	Fat	CHO	NSP	Energy	Energy
	g	g	g	g	g	kcals	kj
Average	82	1.7	7.2	4.5	2.2	87	360

28. PUNJABI COURGETTE CURRY

Average

907g	courgettes	35g	chillies
165g	onions	10g	ginger
153g	tinned tomatoes	8g	garlic
80g	corn oil	(salt)	

Cooked Weight 700g

Lower Fat

1020g	courgettes	75g	corn oil
315g	onions	10g	garlic
230g	tinned tomatoes	5g	ginger
(salt, green chilli)			

Cooked Weight 1106g

Heat oil, add onions and fry. Add garlic, ginger, spices and salt. Add prepared vegetables cut to size and stir. Add tomatoes (or tomato paste), then remaining ingredients and extra water if necessary. Cook to desired consistency.

Nutrient content per 100g cooked weight

	Water	Protein	Fat	CHO	NSP	Energy	Energy
	g	g	g	g	g	kcals	kj
Average	75	3.1	12.0	5.7	1.8	141	585
Lower fat	84	2.3	7.1	4.8	1.4	90	380

Vegetable dishes

29. PUNJABI MARROW CURRY

Average

980g	marrow
56g	tinned tomatoes
42g	oil
(salt)	

14g	ginger
12g	garlic
11g	chillies

Cooked Weight 614g

Heat oil, add onions and fry. Add garlic, ginger spices and salt. Add prepared vegetables cut to size and stir. Add tomatoes (or tomato paste),then remaining ingredients and extra water if necessary. Cook to desired consistency.

Nutrient content per 100g cooked weight

	Water g	Protein g	Fat g	CHO g	NSP g	Energy kcals	Energy kj
Average	84	1.1	7.2	4.5	1.0	85	360

30. PUNJABI CARROT, PEAS, AND POTATO CURRY

Average

690g	carrots
260g	frozen peas
160g	potatoes
112g	onions

68g	butter
11g	chillies
(salt, whole cumin seeds)	

Cooked Weight 1020g

Lower Fat

338g	potatoes
294g	carrots
77g	peas
66g	onions

28g	sunflower oil
16g	ginger
10g	chillies
(salt, whole cumin seeds)	

Cooked Weight 870g

Heat oil and fry cumin seeds followed by chillies. Add chopped onions (and ginger) and stir fry till translucent. Add carrots and peas, stir fry, turn down heat cook till tender. Add boiled potatoes and remaining ingredients, stir and heat through.

Nutrient content per 100g cooked weight

	Water g	Protein g	Fat g	CHO g	NSP g	Energy kcals	Energy kj
Average	77	2.5	6.1	11.3	3.3	105	440
Lower fat	81	1.8	3.6	11.0	1.8	80	335

Vegetable dishes

31. PUNJABI CARROT AND PEAS CURRY

Average

800g	carrots	13g	ginger
210g	frozen peas	5g	chillies
122g	ghee		
(salt, whole cumin, ground turmeric)			

Cooked Weight 920g

Lower Fat

784g	carrots	50g	peas
70g	corn oil	12g	garlic
70g	fresh tomatoes	4g	chillies
(salt, whole cumin, ground turmeric)			

Cooked Weight 750g

Heat oil and fry cumin seeds followed by chillies. Add chopped onions (and ginger) and stir fry till translucent. Add carrots and peas stir fry, turn down heat cook till tender. Add remaining ingredients, stir and heat through.

Nutrient content per 100g cooked weight

	Water	Protein	Fat	CHO	NSP	Energy	Energy
	g	g	g	g	g	kcals	kj
Average	72	1.9	13.8	9.1	3.3	165	685
Lower fat	77	1.3	9.8	9.6	3.0	130	535

32. PUNJABI CARROT AND POTATO CURRY

Average

720g	carrots	80g	sunflower oil
215g	tinned tomatoes	48g	ginger
190g	onions	40g	chillies
110g	potatoes	10g	coriander leaves to garnish
100g	fenugreek		
(salt, whole cumin, ground turmeric)			

Cooked Weight 1150g

Lower Fat

740g	carrots	70g	ghee
280g	onions	60g	chillies
280g	potatoes	20g	ginger
140g	fresh tomatoes		
(salt, whole cumin, ground turmeric)			

Cooked Weight 1270g

Heat oil and fry cumin seeds followed by chillies. Add chopped onions (and ginger) and stir fry till translucent. Add carrots and potatoes, stir fry, add tomatoes , turn down heat cook till tender. Add remaining ingredients, stir and heat through.

Nutrient content per 100g cooked weight

	Water	Protein	Fat	CHO	NSP	Energy	Energy
	g	g	g	g	g	kcals	kj
Average	68	1.9	12.4	15.6	2.4	175	735
Lower fat	80	1.3	5.8	11.1	2.2	100	420

Vegetable dishes

33. PUNJABI GREEN CHILLI AND CARROT

Average

224g	carrots	14g	green chillies
18g	vegetable oil		

(salt, whole cumin, ground turmeric)

Cooked Weight 240g

Lower Fat

390g	carrots	21g	green chillies
20g	vegetable oil		

(salt, whole cumin, ground turmeric)

Cooked Weight 400g

Heat oil, fry chillies and spices if used. Add sliced carrots and stir fry until soft adding a little water if necessary.

Nutrient content per 100g cooked weight

	Water	Protein	Fat	CHO	NSP	Energy	Energy
	g	g	g	g	g	kcals	kj
Average	82	0.7	7.8	8.0	2.4	105	430
Lower fat	85	0.7	5.5	4.6	1.9	70	390

34. PUNJABI CABBAGE (GOBI)

Average

700g	cabbage	25g	soya oil
295g	onions	15g	chillies
35g	ginger		

(salt, ground turmeric, garlic)

Cooked Weight 935g

Heat oil and fry sliced onions. Add ginger, chilli, garlic and turmeric. Add sliced cabbage with water clinging to it. Add salt, cover and cook for 15mins letting liquid evaporate for the last 5 minutes.

Nutrient content per 100g cooked weight

	Water	Protein	Fat	CHO	NSP	Energy	Energy
	g	g	g	g	g	kcals	kj
Average	86	1.8	3.1	6.1	2.3	60	240

Vegetable dishes

35. GUJARATI SAMBARO

Average

143g carrots
141g cabbage
35g corn oil
(salt, black mustard seeds, ground cumin and turmeric, fresh green chilli, chilli powder, lemon juice)

Cooked Weight 300g

Lower Fat

245g cabbage
135g carrots
120g potatoes
20g corn oil

(salt and spices as above)

Cooked Weight 520g

Heat oil and fry mustard seeds with cumin and add green chilli. Put in shredded cabbage and carrots and stir fry for 5 minutes. If potatoes are used add with cabbage and carrots and cook till tender, cut potatoes like chips so that they cook quickly.

Nutrient content per 100g cooked weight

	Water	Protein	Fat	CHO	NSP	Energy	Energy
	g	g	g	g	g	kcals	kj
Average	38	3.2	35.2	16.7	6.7	393	1622
Lower fat	85	1.4	4.2	7.2	1.9	70	295

36. PUNJABI CABBAGE AND POTATO CURRY

Average

738g cabbage   35g chillies
212g onions   30g ginger
170g fresh tomatoes 10g garlic
165g potatoes
100g ghee
(salt, cumin seeds, ground turmeric, garam masala)

Cooked Weight 1070g

Lower Fat

1010g cabbage   40g vegetable oil
318g potatoes   34g ginger
288g onions   20g chillies
78g tomatoes   20g garlic
(salt and spices as above)

Cooked Weight 1300g

Heat oil, add spices and fry. Add prepared potatoes cut to size and stir. Add chopped cabbage, tomatoes, then remaining ingredients and extra water if necessary. Cook to desired consistency.

Nutrient content per 100g cooked weight

	Water	Protein	Fat	CHO	NSP	Energy	Energy
	g	g	g	g	g	kcals	kj
Average	76	2.1	9.8	8.3	2.4	130	530
Lower fat	80	2.1	3.4	10.7	2.4	80	330

Vegetable dishes

37. PUNJABI CABBAGE PEAS AND POTATO CURRY

Average

420g	cabbage	85g	vegetable oil
200g	peas	66g	tomatoes
115g	potatoes	24g	garlic

(salt, cumin seeds, ground turmeric, garam masala)

Cooked Weight 860g

Heat oil, add spices and fry. Add prepared potatoes cut to size and stir. Add chopped cabbage, tomatoes, then remaining ingredients and extra water if necessary. Cook to desired consistency.

Nutrient content per 100g cooked weight

	Water g	Protein g	Fat g	CHO g	NSP g	Energy kcals	Energy kj
Average	73	3.3	10.5	8.4	2.8	140	575

38. PUNJABI CAULIFLOWER CURRY

Average

640g	cauliflower	60g	corn oil
150g	onions	10g	chillies

(salt, cumin seeds)

Cooked Weight 760g

Lower Fat

1045g	cauliflower	12g	ginger
130g	onions	10g	coriander
45g	corn oil	10g	chillies
13g	garlic		(salt, cumin seeds)

Cooked Weight 1265g

Heat oil and fry seeds and garlic. Blend the onions, ginger and chillies in a blender and add to the pan with salt and cauliflower florets and toss to mix thoroughly. Add a little water, cover pan and cook shaking pan occasionally till cauliflower is cooked but still crisp.

Nutrient content per 100g cooked weight

	Water g	Protein g	Fat g	CHO g	NSP g	Energy kcals	Energy kj
Average	79	3.4	8.9	4.1	1.8	105	440
Lower fat	86	3.3	4.5	3.6	1.7	70	285

Vegetable dishes

39. PUNJABI CAULIFLOWER AND POTATO CURRY

Average

1020g cauliflower	105g butter
790g potatoes	5g chillies
155g onions	

(salt, cumin seeds, ground turmeric)

Cooked Weight 1400g

Lower Fat

1180g cauliflower	20g ginger
220g potatoes	19g garlic
125g onions	17g chillies
60g sunflower oil	

(salt, cumin seeds, ground turmeric)

Cooked Weight 1850g

Boil potatoes, drain and cut into cubes. Heat oil and fry seeds and garlic. Blend the onions, ginger and chillies in a blender and add to the pan with salt, cauliflower florets and potatoes and toss to mix thoroughly. Add a little water, cover pan and cook, shaking pan occasionally till cauliflower and potatoes are cooked. (The lower fat version has water added to make a moister consistency).

Nutrient content per 100g cooked weight

	Water	Protein	Fat	CHO	NSP	Energy	Energy
	g	g	g	g	g	kcals	kj
Average	72	4.0	7.0	12.8	2.2	125	525
Lower fat	85	2.8	3.9	4.9	1.4	65	270

40. PUNJABI CAULIFLOWER, TOMATOES AND POTATO CURRY

Average

460g cauliflower	40g ghee
240g tomatoes	23g garlic
200g potatoes	22g ginger
130g onions	10g coriander

(salt, cumin seeds, ground turmeric)

Cooked Weight 790g

Lower Fat

710g cauliflower	50g corn oil
570g potatoes	15g garlic
215g fresh tomatoes	10g ginger
180g onions	

(salt, cumin seeds, ground turmeric)

Cooked Weight 1400g

Boil potatoes, drain and cut into cubes. Heat oil and fry seeds and garlic. Blend the onions, ginger and chillies in a blender and add to the pan with salt, add remaining ingredients and toss to mix thoroughly. Add a little water, cover pan and cook shaking pan occasionally till cauliflower and potatoes are cooked.

Nutrient content per 100g cooked weight

	Water	Protein	Fat	CHO	NSP	Energy	Energy
	g	g	g	g	g	kcals	kj
Average	78	3.5	5.8	9.1	1.9	100	415
Lower fat	79	3.0	4.2	10.3	1.8	90	370

Vegetable dishes

41. PUNJABI RUNNER BEANS AND POTATOES CURRY

Average

640g	runner beans	110g	fresh tomatoes
640g	potatoes	80g	butter
195g	onions	5g	chillies
(salt, cumin seeds, ground turmeric)			

Cooked Weight 1230g

Heat oil, add whole spices and fry. Add prepared vegetables cut to size and fry. Add tomatoes, then remaining ingredients and extra water if necessary. Cook to desired consistency.

Nutrient content per 100g cooked weight

	Water	Protein	Fat	CHO	NSP	Energy	Energy
	g	g	g	g	g	kcals	kj
Average	77	2.3	5.7	12.1	2.0	105	440

42. PUNJABI GOURD (KADDU) CURRY

Average

500g	gourd (bottle)	29g	ginger
229g	canned tomatoes	25g	urad
225g	onions	20g	chillies
80g	ghee	15g	garlic
(salt, cumin seeds, ground turmeric)			

Cooked Weight 610g

Peel and wash gourd and cut into cubes. Heat ghee and add cumin. When it starts to splutter add spices and stir. Add blended paste of onions, garlic and ginger and cook Add gourd, tomatoes, and pre-cooked dhal with some water and cook on a low heat till they are done.

Nutrient content per 100g cooked weight

	Water	Protein	Fat	CHO	NSP	Energy	Energy
	g	g	g	g	g	kcals	kj
Average	71	2.5	13.4	9.1	1.4	165	685

Vegetable dishes

43. PUNJABI GOURD AND POTATO CURRY

Average

410g	gourd
135g	potatoes
68g	tomatoes
60g	vegetable oil
15g	garlic

(salt, cumin seeds, ground turmeric, ginger, green chillies)

Cooked Weight 750g

Lower Fat

660g	gourd
370g	potatoes
350g	tomatoes
325g	onions
55g	margarine
50g	ginger
15g	garlic
10g	chillies

(salt, cumin seeds, ground turmeric)
Cooked Weight 1560g

Peel and wash gourd and cut into cubes. Heat ghee and add cumin. When it starts to splutter add spices and stir. Add blended paste of onions, garlic and ginger and cook. Add gourd, tomatoes, and pre-cooked potatoes with some water and cook on a low heat till vegetables are done.

Nutrient content per 100g cooked weight

	Water g	Protein g	Fat g	CHO g	NSP g	Energy kcals	Energy kj
Average	85	0.9	8.1	5.2	1.8	95	400
Lower fat	86	1.4	3.1	8.3	1.6	65	270

44. GUJARATI DUDHI (GOURD) CURRY

Average

225g	dudhi
30g	oil

(salt, cumin seeds, ground turmeric and chilli, coriander leaves to garnish)

Cooked Weight 440g

Peel and wash gourd and cut into cubes. Heat oil and add cumin. When it starts to splutter add spices and stir. Add gourd and some water and cook on a low heat till they are done. Coriander to garnish.

Nutrient content per 100g cooked weight

	Water g	Protein g	Fat g	CHO g	NSP g	Energy kcals	Energy kj
Average	91	0.2	6.9	1.4	1.6	70	280

45. PUNJABI TINDORA

Average

1200g	tindora	40g	coriander
400g	tinned tomatoes	20g	garlic
320g	corn oil	20g	ginger
(salt, cumin seeds, ground turmeric)		

Cooked Weight 1000g

Lower Fat

1178g	tindora	15g	tomato puree
295g	onions	10g	garlic
135g	oil	8g	ground coriander
40g	ginger	3g	chillies
31g	tinned tomatoes		

Cooked Weight 1230g

Peel and wash tindora and cut into cubes. Heat ghee and add cumin. When it starts to splutter add spices and stir.
Add blended paste of (onions), garlic and ginger and cook.
Add tindora, tomatoes and cook on a low heat till vegetables are done.

Nutrient content per 100g cooked weight

	Water	Protein	Fat	CHO	NSP	Energy	Energy
	g	g	g	g	g	kcals	kj
Average	57	2.4	32.3	6.1	3.4	325	1335
Lower fat	78	1.9	11.3	6.0	3.0	130	540

46. GUJARATI TINDORA CURRY

Average

420g	tindora	2g	cumin
100g	mixed vegetable oil	2g	turmeric
(salt, cumin seeds, ground coriander, chilli)		

Cooked Weight 155g

Wash and cut the tindora into four lengthwise. Heat oil and add cumin seeds. When it starts to splutter add spices and stir. Add tindora and some water and cook on a low heat, uncovered, till cooked.

Nutrient content per 100g cooked weight

	Water	Protein	Fat	CHO	NSP	Energy	Energy
	g	g	g	g	g	kcals	kj
Average	58	2.1	32.8	4.9	3.5	320	1315

Vegetable dishes

47. GUJARATI TURIA (RIDGE GOURD) AND POTATO CURRY

Average

1000g	turia (ridge gourd)	100g	oil
640g	potatoes	4g	chilli powder
390g	tinned tomatoes	2g	turmeric

(salt, mustard and fenugreek seeds, ground cumin, coriander, garlic)

Cooked Weight 1960g

Lower Fat

630g	turia	(salt and spices as above)
270g	tomatoes	
150g	potatoes	
50g	corn oil	

Cooked Weight 1100g

Wash turia and cut off the ridges. Cut into cubes. Peel and wash potatoes and cut into cubes. Heat oil and fry mustard seeds, fenugreek and chopped garlic. Add tomatoes and the rest of the spices. Stir for a while and then add the potatoes and turia. Cover and cook on a low heat till the vegetables are done.

Nutrient content per 100g cooked weight

	Water	Protein	Fat	CHO	NSP	Energy	Energy
	g	g	g	g	g	kcals	kj
Average	84	1.3	5.3	7.9	1.8	80	340
Lower fat	87	0.9	4.7	5.0	1.6	65	270

48. PUNJABI KARELA

Average

268g	karela	8g	ginger
132g	spring onions	2g	garlic
100g	tomatoes		
51g	corn oil		

(salt, jaggery, green chillies, lemon juice, garam masala, chopped coriander)

Cooked Weight 373g

Lower Fat

630g	karela	50g	ghee
420g	onions	10g	chillies
250g	tinned tomatoes		

(salt, ginger, garlic, lemon juice, garam masala, chopped coriander)

Cooked Weight 1150g

Soak karela in salted water. Drain, slice and fry in oil (or ghee). Put aside and in the same oils. Fry chopped onions, garlic, ginger and green chillies. Add lemon juice and sugar then fried karela. Cook for about 15mins. Garnish with garam masala and chopped coriander.

Nutrient content per 100g cooked weight

	Water	Protein	Fat	CHO	NSP	Energy	Energy
	g	g	g	g	g	kcals	kj
Average	75	2.1	14.1	3.8	2.7	150	615
Lower fat	74	1.6	4.5	4.1	2.1	60	250

Vegetable dishes

49. GUJARATI KARELA (BITTER GOURD)

Average

270g karela
60g   oil
(salt, cumin seeds, ground turmeric, coriander and cumin, chilli, jaggery)

Cooked weight 620g

Scrape the ridges off the karela and cut into rings. Rub with about a tablespoon of salt and let stand for about an hour. Wash with plenty of water removing the seeds. Heat oil, add cumin seeds and fry karela. Add spices, stir and cook on low heat.

Nutrient content per 100g cooked weight

	Water	Protein	Fat	CHO	NSP	Energy	Energy
	g	g	g	g	g	kcals	kj
Average	90	1.0	6.3	0.5	1.7	65	270

50. GUJARATI GUWAR

Average

240g guwar beans
170g tomatoes
70g   ground nut oil
15g   garlic
(salt, ajma seeds, ground turmeric, coriander, cumin and chilli)

Cooked Weight 390g

Wash, top and tail guwar. Boil with a little salt till cooked. Drain and leave aside. Heat a little oil and add ajma, garlic cut into pieces and tomatoes with the rest of the spices. Stir till everything is well blended and add guwar. Cook on low heat.

Nutrient content per 100g cooked weight

	Water	Protein	Fat	CHO	NSP	Energy	Energy
	g	g	g	g	g	kcals	kj
Average	70	2.3	18.1	3.8	2.9	190	770

Vegetable dishes

51. GUJARATI MOOLI BHAJI

Average

420g	mooli	2g	green chillies
50g	oil	1g	fenugreek (methi)
31g	gram flour	1g	mustard seeds
9g	salt	1g	turmeric

Cooked Weight 382g

Wash the mooli and cut into thin slices. Save the leaves. Heat oil and add mustard seeds, then fenugreek. Add the chilli, cut in half. Add spices, stir and add sliced mooli and the leaves. Rub a little oil into the gram flour and set it on top of the vegetables in the pan. Cook slowly till mooli is cooked and all the water has evaporated. Mix everything together, including the cooked flour.

Nutrient content per 100g cooked weight

	Water	Protein	Fat	CHO	NSP	Energy	Energy
		g	g	g	g	kcals	kj
Average	69	2.6	13.9	7.2	1.9	160	665

52. PUNJABI PEA AND POTATO CURRY

Average

610g	peas	140g	butter
298g	potatoes	33g	ginger
288g	tomatoes	31g	chillies
150g	onion		

(salt, whole cumin, green/red chilli, ground turmeric garam masala, coriander leaves to garnish)

Cooked Weight 2410g

Lower Fat

278g	potatoes	28g	sunflower oil
124g	peas	11g	ginger
82g	tomatoes	7g	chillies
76g	onions		

(salt and spices as above)

Cooked Weight 798g

Peel potatoes and cut into cubes. Heat oil, add cumin seeds. Add tomatoes, sliced garlic and spices. When well blended add peas, cook till they begin to soften and add potatoes. Cook till done.

Nutrient content per 100g cooked weight

	Water	Protein	Fat	CHO	NSP	Energy	Energy
		g	g	g	g	kcals	kj
Average	84	2.3	5.2	6.1	1.6	80	330
Lower fat	84	1.8	3.8	8.7	1.5	75	310

Pulse Dishes

Pulse dishes

53. GUJARATI PEAS AND POTATO CURRY

Average

194g	peas
160g	potatoes
148g	tomatoes
50g	vegetable oil

(salt, cumin and mustard seeds, ground turmeric, coriander, cumin and chilli)

Cooked Weight 596 g

Lower Fat

275g	potatoes
215g	frozen peas
80g	tomatoes
15g	corn oil

(salt and spices as above)

Cooked Weight 660g

Peel potatoes and cut into cubes. Heat oil, add cumin and mustard seeds. Add tomatoes and spices. When well blended add peas, cook till they begin to get soft and add potatoes and water if needed. Cook till done.

Nutrient content per 100g cooked weight

	Water	Protein	Fat	CHO	NSP	Energy	Energy
	g	g	g	g	g	kcals	kj
Average	74	3.3	9.7	9.8	2.2	135	565
Lower fat	81	2.8	2.7	10.1	2.3	75	315

54. PUNJABI MASUR DHAL WITH ONION

Average

| 350g | masur | 54g | corn oil |
| 215g | onions | 10g | garlic |

(salt, cumin seeds, ginger, ground turmeric)

Cooked Weight 1295g

Lower Fat

175g	masur	15g	garlic
90g	onions	15g	ginger
20g	ghee		

(salt, cumin seeds, ground turmeric)

Cooked Weight 1040g

Boil masur dhal with water and salt until tender. Fry cumin seeds in oil or ghee then add onions, garlic and ginger and fry. Add to the cooked dhal with remaining ingredients and water. Cook until flavours are combined.

Nutrient content per 100g cooked weight

	Water	Protein	Fat	CHO	NSP	Energy	Energy
	g	g	g	g	g	kcals	kj
Average	70	6.7	4.6	16.6	1.6	130	545
Lower fat	81	4.3	2.2	10.5	1.0	75	320

Pulse dishes

55. PUNJABI MASUR DHAL WITH TOMATO AND ONION

Average

275g	masur	80g	tomatoes
90g	onions	38g	chillies
80g	butter		

(salt, cumin seeds, ginger, ground turmeric)

Cooked Weight 1560g

Lower fat

155g	masur	8g	garlic
155g	tinned tomatoes	8g	ginger
80g	onions	8g	soya oil
12g	coriander	4g	chilli

(salt, cumin seeds, ginger, ground turmeric)

Cooked Weight: 980g

Boil masur dhal with water and salt until tender. Fry cumin seeds in oil or ghee then add onions, garlic and ginger and fry. Add to the cooked dhal with remaining ingredients and water. Cook until flavours are combined.

Nutrient content per 100g cooked weight

	Water	Protein	Fat	CHO	NSP	Energy	Energy
	g	g	g	g	g	kcals	kj
Average	79	4.4	4.5	10.6	1.0	100	410
Lower fat	82	4.1	1.1	10.3	1.1	65	275

56. PUNJABI MASUR DHAL (THICK)

Average

1410g	masur	10g	ginger
75g	ghee	9g	garlic
11g	chilli		

(salt, cumin seeds , ground turmeric)

Cooked Weight 2130g

Boil masur dhal with water and salt until tender. Fry cumin seeds in oil or ghee then add onions, garlic and ginger and fry. Add to the cooked dhal with remaining ingredients and water. Cook until flavours are combined.

Nutrient content per 100g cooked weight

	Water	Protein	Fat	CHO	NSP	Energy	Energy
	g	g	g	g	g	kcals	kj
Average	38	15.8	4.4	37.4	3.3	240	1030

57. PUNJABI MASUR AND MUNG DHAL

Average

225g	masur	77g	onions
225g	mung	28g	chilli
102g	butter	7g	garlic
80g	tomatoes	7g	ginger

(salt, cumin seeds, ground turmeric)

Cooked Weight 1960g

Lower Fat

190g	mung	30g	ghee
190g	masur	25g	ginger
80g	onions	15g	garlic
50g	tomatoes	15g	chilli

(salt, cumin seeds , ground turmeric)

Cooked Weight 2140g

Boil dhals with water and salt until tender. Fry cumin seeds in oil or ghee then add onions, garlic and ginger and fry. Add to the cooked dhal with remaining ingredients and water. Cook until flavours are combined.

Nutrient content per 100g cooked weight

	Water	Protein	Fat	CHO	NSP	Energy	Energy
	g	g	g	g	g	kcals	kj
Average	74	6.0	4.6	12.5	1.8	110	470
Lower fat	81	4.5	1.7	9.9	1.5	70	295

58. PUNJABI MIXED DHAL (MASUR, MUNG, CHANNA.)

Average

172g	masur	65g	fresh tomatoes
146g	mung	40g	ghee
120g	onions	10g	ginger
100g	channa	6g	chilli

(salt, garlic, cumin seeds, ground turmeric)

Cooked Weight 1100g

Lower Fat

150g	mung	45g	chillies
145g	tinned tomatoes	25g	coriander
135g	masur	25g	ghee
120g	channa	25g	ginger
80g	onions	15g	garlic

(salt)

Cooked Weight 2510g

Boil dhals with and salt until tender. Fry cumin seeds, then onions in oil or ghee, add spices and fry. Add with the remaining ingredients to the cooked dhals and water. Cook until flavours are combined. Garnish with coriander if used.

Nutrient content per 100g cooked weight

	Water	Protein	Fat	CHO	NSP	Energy	Energy
		g	g	g	g	kcals	kj
Average	60	9.6	4.6	20.6	3.3	155	660
Lower fat	85	4.1	1.4	9.2	1.5	65	270

Pulse dishes

59. PAKISTANI MASOOR DHAL (RED SPLIT LENTILS)

Average

264g	masoor dhal	3g	turmeric
62g	butter ghee	3g	salt
20g	garlic	2g	cumin powder
3g	coriander powder	1g	dry green chillies

Cooked Weight 1050g

Boil dhal with salt, chilli powder, dried coriander, and turmeric until soft. Heat ghee in a frying pan with garlic and spices and add to dhal.

Nutrient content per 100g cooked weight

	Water	Protein	Fat	CHO	NSP	Energy	Energy
		g	g	g	g	kcals	kj
Average	70	6.2	6.3	14.5	0.9	135	565

60. BENGALI MASOOR DHAL

Average

148g	masoor dhal	16g	garlic
58g	onions	8g	green chillies
24g	corn oil	2g	turmeric
10g	lemon juice	1g	coriander powder
12g	salt		

Cooked Weight 938g

Boil lentils and mash. Add rest of the spices. Save some coriander for garnish. Separately fry onions and garlic and add to the dhal mixture.

Lower fat

182g	masoor dhal	8g	butter ghee
100g	onions	8g	fresh coriander
24g	corn oil	4g	dry chillies
16g	salt	2g	turmeric
10g	garlic		

Soak dhal for a few hours. Boil with salt, onions and turmeric. Fry onion, garlic and red chillies in ghee and when brown add to the lentils. Garnish with coriander.

Nutrient content per 100g cooked weight

	Water	Protein	Fat	CHO	NSP	Energy	Energy
		g	g	g	g	g	kcals	kj
Average	80	4.0	2.8	9.7	0.9	75	325
Lower fat	87	2.9	0.7	7.2	0.7	45	190

61. PUNJABI CHANNA DHAL (THIN)

Average

700g	white chick peas (channa)	30g	garlic
110g	onions	30g	ginger
36g	ghee		(salt, ground turmeric)

Cooked Weight 2400g

Lower Fat

560g	white channa	35g	ginger
344g	onions	18g	garlic
	(salt, ground turmeric)		

Cooked Weight 1817g

Soak channa overnight and boil until tender. Fry onions in ghee with crushed garlic and chopped ginger. Add turmeric then add channa and cooking water and cook until done.

Nutrient content per 100g cooked weight

	Water	Protein	Fat	CHO	NSP	Energy	Energy
		g	g	g	g	kcals	kj
Average	71	6.4	3.1	15.2	3.2	110	465
Lower fat	70	6.9	1.7	17.1	3.6	110	465

62. PUNJABI CHANNA DHAL (THICK)

Average

785g	channa	42g	onions
98g	ghee	7g	ginger
	(salt, ground turmeric)		

Cooked Weight 1500 g

Lower Fat

250g	channa	25g	chilli
200g	onions	20g	garlic
35g	corn oil	20g	ginger
	(salt, ground turmeric)		

Cooked Weight 800g

Soak channa overnight and boil until tender. Fry onions in ghee with crushed garlic and chopped ginger. Add turmeric then add channa and cooking water and cook until done.

Nutrient content per 100g cooked weight

	Water	Protein	Fat	CHO	NSP	Energy	Energy
		g	g	g	g	kcals	kj
Average	42	13	10.2	28.8	6.2	250	1060
Lower fat	62	8	6.2	19.2	3.8	160	670

Pulse dishes

63. PUNJABI CHANNA DHAL WITH TOMATO

Average

536g	channa	136g	corn oil
400g	tinned tomatoes	42g	ginger
260g	onions	9g	garlic
(salt, ground turmeric)			

Cooked Weight 2900g

Lower Fat

300g	split chickpeas	32g	chillies
95g	onions	28g	ginger
65g	butter	25g	garlic
64g	tomatoes	(salt, ground turmeric)	

Cooked Weight 1746g

Soak channa overnight and boil until tender. Fry onions in butter with crushed garlic, chillies and chopped ginger. Add turmeric, then add channa, tomatoes and cooking water and cook until done.

Nutrient content per 100g cooked weight

	Water	Protein	Fat	CHO	NSP	Energy	Energy
	g	g	g	g	g	kcals	kj
Average	77	4.5	5.6	10.5	2.2	110	450
Lower fat	81	4.2	3.5	9.6	2.1	85	355

64. PUNJABI WHOLE CHICKPEAS

Average

1760g	chickpeas	66g	tomato puree
540g	onions	29g	ginger
151g	coriander leaves	5g	green chilli
95g	corn oil	(salt, ground turmeric, lemon juice garam masala)	

Cooked Weight 3780g

Lower Fat

820g	chickpeas	30g	sunflower oil
230g	onions	8g	chilli
120g	tomatoes	(salt, ground turmeric, lemon juice, coriander leaves)	

Soak chickpeas overnight. Drain and cook in salted fresh water until tender (20mins in a pressure cooker). Fry onion and ginger till golden, add turmeric, and fry. Then add chilli, garam masala, tomatoes and half the coriander. Add chickpeas and stir well then add cooking liquid and simmer till tender. Add lemon juice and sprinkle with remaining coriander.

Cooked Weight 3164g

Nutrient content per 100g cooked weight

	Water	Protein	Fat	CHO	NSP	Energy	Energy
	g	g	g	g	g	kcals	kj
Average	53	10.3	5.1	24.6	5.1	180	775
Lower fat	75	5.6	2.4	13.5	2.9	75	315

Pulse dishes

65. PUNJABI CHANNA ALOO (WHOLE CHICKPEA AND POTATO)

Average

480g	whole black channa	135g	corn oil
450g	onions	90g	ginger
450g	potatoes	35g	garlic
397g	tinned tomatoes	30g	chilli
		(salt, ground turmeric)	

Cooked Weight 1377g

Lower Fat

400g	tinned tomatoes	100g	vegetable ghee
285g	potatoes	35g	ginger
265g	whole black channa	15g	coriander
245g	onion	(salt, ground turmeric)	

Cooked Weight 2400g

Soak chick peas overnight, cook until tender. Boil potatoes and cut into small pieces. Heat oil and fry whole spices and then onions, garlic and ginger. Add tomatoes, salt and ground spices. Stir to blend, add potatoes and chickpeas and cook for a few minutes.

Nutrient content per 100g cooked weight

	Water	Protein	Fat	CHO	NSP	Energy	Energy
	g	g	g	g	g	kcals	kj
Average	45	9.1	11.8	27.5	5.0	245	1030
Lower fat	81	2.9	4.8	8.9	1.6	90	370

66. PUNJABI CHANA AND URAD DHAL

Average

175g	channa	50g	butter
175g	urad	5g	chillies
90g	onions	5g	garlic
(salt, cumin seeds, ground turmeric)			

Cooked Weight 1690g

Soak channa overnight. Boil dhals with water and salt until tender. Fry cumin seeds in oil or ghee then add onions, garlic and ginger and fry. Add to the cooked dhal with remaining ingredients and water. Cook until flavours are combined.

Nutrient content per 100g cooked weight

	Water	Protein	Fat	CHO	NSP	Energy	Energy
	g	g	g	g	g	kcals	kj
Average	78	5.1	3.2	9.8	2.6	85	360

Pulse dishes

67. PAKISTANI CHANNA DHAL

Average

230g	split chick peas (channa)
110g	tomatoes
68g	onions
54g	butter ghee
14g	ginger

10g	garlic
2g	chilli powder
1g	gara masala
1g	salt

Cooked Weight 1064g

Lower Fat

800g	boiled chickpeas
174g	onions
100g	tinned tomatoes
20g	sunflower oil
20g	garlic

10g	chilli powder
10g	cumin
10g	garam masala
10g	ginger
10g	salt

Cooked Weight 1164g

Soak channa overnight. Fry onions in ghee with crushed garlic add ginger and spices. When onions are brown add water and tomatoes and cook. Add channa and water cook in a pressure cooker till done.

Nutrient content per 100g cooked weight

	Water	Protein	Fat	CHO	NSP	Energy	Energy
	g	g	g	g	g	kcals	kj
Average	73	5.1	6.2	11.6	1.8	120	500
Low fat	67	6.6	3.8	15.4	1.9	115	480

68. PAKISTANI CHICK PEA (AND POTATO) CURRY

Average

241g	boiled chick peas
125g	tinned tomatoes
120g	potatoes
56g	chopped onions
50g	corn oil
6g	garam masala

5g	fresh coriander
5g	salt
4g	garlic
4g	ginger
2g	turmeric
2g	green chillies

Cooked Weight 610g

Fry onions, garlic, and ginger. Add tomatoes and spices. Add potatoes and water. Cook then add boiled chick peas. Garnish with coriander.

Nutrient content per 100g cooked weight

	Water	Protein	Fat	CHO	NSP	Energy	Energy
	g	g	g	g	g	kcals	kj
Average	69	4.4	9.3	12.9	2.3	150	625

69. PUNJABI MUNG DHAL

Average

600g	mung dhal	29g	tomato puree
234g	onions	6g	garlic
78g	ghee	4g	chilli
32g	coriander		

(salt, cumin seeds, ground turmeric)

Cooked Weight 2840g

Lower Fat

240g	mung dhal	55g	onions
120g	tomatoes	5g	sunflower oil

(salt, cumin seeds, ground turmeric)

Cooked Weight 800g

Boil dhal with salt until tender. Fry cumin seeds, then onions in oil or ghee, add spices and fry. Add with the remaining ingredients to the cooked dhal and water. Cook until flavours are combined.

Nutrient content per 100g cooked weight

	Water	Protein	Fat	CHO	NSP	Energy	Energy
	g	g	g	g	g	kcals	kj
Average	77	5.9	3.0	10.6	2.3	90	380
Lower fat	73	8.2	1.1	14.9	3.2	100	420

70. PUNJABI WHOLE MUNG DHAL

Average

240g	mung	13g	garlic
75g	onions	12g	coriander
66g	butter	11g	chilli
17g	ginger		(salt, turmeric)

Cooked Weight 1579g

Lower Fat

315g	mung	6g	chilli
75g	onions	6g	ginger
35g	ghee		(salt, turmeric)

Cooked Weight 1630g

Wash and soak mung for 3 hours. Fry onions in half butter or ghee till soft, add garlic and ginger and fry. Add mung beans, turmeric and salt. Cook on low heat till beans are tender, add remaining butter, stir and serve .

Nutrient content per 100g cooked weight

	Water	Protein	Fat	CHO	NSP	Energy	Energy
	g	g	g	g	g	kcals	kj
Average	82	3.8	3.6	7.7	1.6	75	320
Low fat	83	4.7	2.1	9.3	2.0	70	305

Pulse dishes

71. PUNJABI WHOLE MUNG CURRY (MUNG WITH TOMATO)

Average

200g	mung
200g	tinned tomatoes
125g	corn oil
100g	onions

15g	coriander
13g	ginger
12g	garlic
(salt)	

Cooked Weight 1517g

Lower Fat

200g	mung
200g	tinned tomatoes
100g	onions
15g	coriander

10g	garlic
10g	ginger
10g	soya oil
5g	chilli
(salt)	

Cooked Weight 1400g

Wash and soak mung for an hour. Boil and set aside. Chop onions and fry till soft. Add tomatoes with the spices and cook till everything is well blended. Add mung and cook on low heat.

Nutrient content per 100g cooked weight

	Water	Protein	Fat	CHO	NSP	Energy	Energy
	g	g	g	g	g	kcals	kj
Average	78	3.6	8.4	7.5	2.9	120	495
Lower fat	84	3.8	1.0	8.0	1.7	55	330

72. PUNJABI MUNG AND MASUR DHAL

Average

150g	mung
80g	masur
75g	onions
(salt, cumin seeds, ground turmeric)	

35g	ghee
7g	chilli

Cooked Weight 1140g

Boil dhal with salt until tender. Fry cumin seeds, then onions in oil or ghee, add spices and fry. Mix this with the remaining ingredients to the cooked dhal and water. Cook until flavours are combined.

Nutrient content per 100g cooked weight

	Water	Protein	Fat	CHO	NSP	Energy	Energy
	g	g	g	g	g	kcals	kj
Average	78	5.4	3.4	10.6	3.0	90	380

73. GUJARATI WHOLE MUNG CURRY

Average

200g	whole mung
360g	tomatoes
105g	onions
55g	ghee

(salt, cumin seeds, ground turmeric, coriander and cumin, green chilli paste, garlic and ginger paste)

Cooked weight 1400g

Wash and soak mung for an hour. Boil and set aside. Chop onions and fry till soft. Add tomatoes with the spices and cook till everything is well blended. Add mung and cook on low heat.

Nutrient content per 100g cooked weight

	Water	Protein	Fat	CHO	NSP	Energy	Energy
	g	g	g	g	g	kcals	kJ
Average	73	5.3	5.8	11.2	2.4	115	480

74. PAKISTANI MUNG DHAL

Average

362g	mung dhal
90g	mixed vegetable oil
32g	onions
18g	garlic
16g	ginger
10g	green chillies
8g	salt
7g	chilli powder
5g	fresh coriander
2g	turmeric

Cooked Weight 1892g

Boil dhal until soft. Fry remaining ingredients in oil and add to dhal. Garnish with coriander.

Nutrient content per 100g cooked weight

	Water	Protein	Fat	CHO	NSP	Energy	Energy
		g	g	g	g	kcals	kJ
Average	77	5.3	5.1	9.2	1.7	100	142

Pulse dishes

75. ISMAILI WHOLE MUNG CURRY

Average

158g	whole dried mung	
140g	onions	
64g	sunflower oil	
78g	tinned tomatoes	
56g	tomato puree	

4g	coriander powder
4g	cumin powder
2g	salt
2g	fresh garlic
2g	chilli powder

Cooked Weight 1160g

Boil mung in salted water until cooked. Fry onions and spices. Add tomatoes and fry. Add boiled, drained mung.

Low Fat

308g	whole dried mung
275g	onions
172g	tinned tomatoes
30g	corn oil
10g	garlic

6g	green chillies
3g	coriander powder
2g	salt
2g	cumin powder
2g	turmeric powder
2g	chilli powder

Cooked Weight 2300g

Nutrient content per 100g cooked weight

	Water	Protein	Fat	CHO	NSP	Energy	Energy
	g	g	g	g	g	kcals	kj
Average	76	4.2	5.9	8.1	1.7	100	420
Lower fat	84	3.5	1.6	7.5	1.6	55	230

76. PUNJABI URAD DHAL

Average

270g	onions
170g	urad
60g	ghee
	(salt, cumin seeds, ground turmeric)

25g	ginger
10g	chilli

Cooked Weight 1884g

Boil dhal with salt until tender. Fry cumin seeds, then onions in oil or ghee, add spices and fry. Add, with the remaining ingredients, to the cooked dhal and water. Cook until flavours are combined.

Nutrient content per 100g cooked weight

	Water	Protein	Fat	CHO	NSP	Energy	Energy
		g	g	g	g	kcals	kj
Average	87	2.5	3.4	5.0	0.9	60	250

77. PUNJABI URAD/TOMATO DHAL

Average

280g	urad	42g	ginger
98g	tomatoes	40g	chillies
95g	onions	35g	garlic
85g	butter		

(salt, cumin seeds, ground turmeric)

Cooked Weight 1694g

Lower Fat

260g	urad	10g	ginger
40g	soya oil	10g	onions
20g	tomato puree		

(salt, cumin seeds, ground turmeric)

Cooked Weight 1830g

Boil dhal with salt until tender. Fry cumin seeds, then onions in oil or ghee, add spices and fry. Add with the remaining ingredients to the cooked dhal and water. Cook until flavours are combined.

Nutrient content per 100g cooked weight

	Water	Protein	Fat	CHO	NSP	Energy	Energy
	g	g	g	g	g	kcals	kj
Average	79	4.5	4.4	8.2	1.6	90	380
Low fat	85	3.9	2.4	6.5	1.5	65	270

78. PUNJABI MUNG AND MOTH DHAL

Average

200g	moth	23g	ginger
200g	mung	19g	chilli
126g	margarine	10g	garlic
54g	onions		

(salt, cumin seeds, ground turmeric)

Cooked Weight 1980g

Lower Fat

198g	mung	75g	ghee
155g	moth	35g	chilli
85g	onions	20g	ginger

(salt , cumin seeds, ground turmeric)

Cooked Weight 2630g

Boil dhals with salt until tender. Fry cumin seeds, then onions in margarine or ghee, add spices and fry. Add with the remaining ingredients to the cooked dhal and water. Cook until flavours are combined.

Nutrient content per 100g cooked weight

	Water	Protein	Fat	CHO	NSP	Energy	Energy
	g	g	g	g	g	kcals	kj
Average	75	5.5	5.6	9.4	2.0	110	450
Lower fat	86	3.6	3.0	6.4	1.2	65	275

Pulse dishes

79. PUNJABI WHOLE MOTH DHAL

Average

500g moth dhal	25g chillies
470g tinned tomatoes	18g garlic
245g onions	17g ginger
120g ghee	

(salt, cumin seeds, ground turmeric)

Cooked Weight: 3257g

Lower Fat

526g moth dhal	70g ghee
230g tomatoes	66g ginger
192g garlic	20g chilli
146g onions	

(salt, cumin seeds, ground turmeric)

Cooked Weight: 4970g

Boil dhals with salt until tender. Fry cumin seeds, then onions in margarine or ghee, add spices and fry. Add with the remaining ingredients to the cooked dhal and water. Cook until flavours are combined.

Nutrient content per 100g cooked weight

	Water	Protein	Fat	CHO	NSP	Energy	Energy
	g	g	g	g	g	kcals	kj
Average	81	4.4	3.9	7.5	1.6	80	340
Lower fat	85	3.5	1.6	6.5	1.4	55	230

80. PAKISTANI DHAL MAASH (BLACK URAD)

Average

418g urad	15g ginger
160g onions	8g coriander powder
80g corn oil	8g chilli powder
17g garlic	5g turmeric

Cooked Weight 1660g

Lower Fat

332g urad	12g garlic
150g tinned tomatoes	12g salt
25g corn oil	2g cumin
12g curry powder	

Cooked Weight 1128g

Soak dhal for a few hours. Brown onions, add garlic and spices add dhal with ginger and water and simmer.

Nutrient content per 100g cooked weight

	Water	Protein	Fat	CHO	NSP	Energy	Energy
	g	g	g	g	g	kcals	kj
Average	69	6.9	5.5	11.9	2.3	125	520
Lower fat	69	7.7	2.8	12.9	2.8	105	450

Pulse dishes

81. PUNJABI TOOR DHAL

Average

244g	toor dhal	60g	vegetable oil
136g	tomatoes	11g	chilli

(salt, cumin seeds, ground turmeric)

Cooked Weight 1420g

Boil dhals with salt until tender. Fry cumin seeds, then onions in margarine or ghee, add spices and fry. Add with the remaining ingredients to the cooked dhal and water. Cook until flavours are combined.

Nutrient content per 100g cooked weight

	Water	Protein	Fat	CHO	NSP	Energy	Energy
	g	g	g	g	g	kcals	kj
Average	80	3.9	4.6	10.4	2.0	95	400

82. GUJARATI TUWAR DHAL (PIGEON PEAS)

Average

220g	pigeon peas
70g	tomatoes
15g	corn oil

(salt, mustard and fenugreek seeds, hing, ground turmeric, chilli and garam masala, jaggery)

Cooked Weight 1280g

Lower Fat

135g	pigeon peas
55g	tomatoes
5g	cotton seed oil

(salt and spices as above)

Cooked Weight 1570g

Boil the dhal till cooked, whisk with the water in which it was boiled and set aside. Heat the oil and add mustard, fenugreek and hing. Add tomatoes and spices, stir for a few minutes and add the whisked dhal. Add water to make desired consistency. At this stage add jaggery and boil, stirring all the time, for 10 minutes.

Nutrient content per 100g cooked weight

	Water	Protein	Fat	CHO	NSP	Energy	Energy
	g	g	g	g	g	kcals	kj
Average	83	3.8	1.5	10.2	0.9	65	280
Lower fat	91	1.9	0.5	5.2	1.0	30	135

Pulse dishes

83. GUJARATI TUWAR (PIGEON PEAS) AND AUBERGINE CURRY

Average

210g	pigeon peas	4g	cumin
255g	aubergines	2g	turmeric
140g	oil		
(salt, ground coriander and chilli)			

Cooked Weight 900g

Lower Fat

286g	pigeon peas	10g	salt
188g	aubergines	2g	cumin
41g	oil	1g	turmeric
(salt and spices as above)			

Cooked Weight 575g

Cut aubergines into cubes. Heat oil and add cumin. Add aubergine and cook for 5 minutes. Add pigeon peas and cook again for 5 mins. Add the spices and cook on low heat adding water if necessary

Nutrient content per 100g cooked weight

	Water	Protein	Fat	CHO	NSP	Energy	Energy
	g	g	g	g	g	kcals	kj
Average	61	4.9	16.1	14.3	2.6	220	910
Lower fat	52	9.7	6.9	25.8	5.2	195	830

84. ISMAILI DHAL

Average

216g	peeled tomatoes	6g	mustard seeds
172g	tuwar dhal	6g	salt
98g	masoor dhal	4g	coriander powder
26g	mix vegetable oil	4g	cumin powder
18g	crushed garlic	2g	fenugreek
14g	fresh coriander		

Cooked Weight 1667g

Cook the dhals in the pressure cooker and liquidise. Heat oil and add mustard seeds until they pop. Add garlic and fry. Add all the other ingredients and cook until oil rises to the top. Pour on to liquidised mixture and mix.

Nutrient content per 100g cooked weight

	Water	Protein	Fat	CHO	NSP	Energy	Energy
		g	g	g	g	kcals	kj
Average	82	4.1	2.1	9.9	0.8	70	295

Pulse dishes

85. PUNJABI SOYA BEAN DHAL

Average

380g	soya beans	15g	ginger
220g	onions	10g	chilli
90g	ghee	10g	garlic
20g	tomatoes		

(salt, cumin seeds, ground turmeric)

Cooked Weight 1210g

Lower Fat

550g	soya beans	70g	corn oil
220g	onions	25g	ginger
220g	tomatoes		

(salt, garlic, cumin seeds, ground turmeric)

Cooked Weight 1550g

Soak soya beans for 20 mins in cold water and drain. Boil with water and salt until tender. Fry cumin seeds, then onions, in oil or ghee, add spices and fry. Add with the remaining ingredients to the cooked dhal and water. Cook until flavours are combined.

Nutrient content per 100g cooked weight

	Water	Protein	Fat	CHO	NSP	Energy	Energy
	g	g	g	g	g	kcals	kj
Average	61	11.6	13.3	6.8	5.3	190	795
Lower fat	61	13.0	10.0	7.3	5.9	170	700

86. PUNJABI KHADI

Average

250g	yogurt	5g	chilli
50g	ghee	5g	ginger
30g	gram flour		

(salt, turmeric, whole garam masala)

Cooked Weight 680g

Lower Fat

50g	gram flour	2g	chillies
50	yogurt	2g	garlic
4g	ginger		

(salt, turmeric, whole garammasala)

Cooked Weight 250g

Fry onions and spices. Mix yogurt with gram flour and water. Add the mixture to the spices. Boil, stirring all the time.

Nutrient content per 100g cooked weight

	Water	Protein	Fat	CHO	NSP	Energy	Energy
	g	g	g	g	g	kcals	kj
Average	82	3.0	8.7	5.2	0.5	110	455
Lower fat	78	5.2	1.7	11.9	2.2	80	340

Pulse dishes

87. GUJARATI KAHDI

Average

1070g buttermilk
60g chick pea flour
(salt, cumin, mustard and fenugreek seeds, curry leaves,
cloves, ground turmeric, green chilli, garlic and ginger
paste, jaggery)

40g ghee

Cooked Weight 1970g

Lower Fat

300g yogurt
20g chick pea flour
(salt and spices as above)

15g ghee
5g jaggery

Cooked Weight 340g

Mix together buttermilk (or yogurt) chickpea flour, chilli paste, turmeric and salt. Heat ghee and add whole spices. Add the buttermilk mixture and stir constantly till it boils. Add jaggery, stir and remove from heat.

Nutrient content per 100g cooked weight

	Water	Protein	Fat	CHO	NSP	Energy	Energy
	g	g	g	g	g	kcals	kj
Average	87	2.3	2.2	8.6	0.3	60	260
Lower fat	88	3.3	0.6	6.4	0.4	45	180

88. ISMAILI KHADI

Average

426g whole milk yogurt
28g gram flour
70g onions
20g mix vegetable oil
14g crushed garlic
8g salt

8g coriander
6g crushed ginger
4g cumin powder
2g cloves
2g mustard seeds
2g fenugreek
2g turmeric

Cooked Weight 1156g

Fry onions and spices. Mix yogurt with gram flour and water. Add the mixture to the spices. Boil, stirring all the time.

Nutrient content per 100g cooked weight

	Water	Protein	Fat	CHO	NSP	Energy	Energy
	g	g	g	g	g	kcals	kj
Average	88	2.6	3.1	4.4	0.4	50	205

Pulse dishes

89. PAKISTANI KHADI

Average

425g	plain yogurt	14g	salt
164g	onions	8g	chilli powder
105g	corn oil	8g	ground coriander
102g	gram flour	2g	turmeric

Cooked Weight 740g

Whisk yogurt and gram flour with spices and water and heat stirring constantly until thick. Fry onions and add to mixture.

Lower Fat

425g	low fat yogurt	15g	fresh coriander
412g	potatoes	13g	curry powder
186g	onions	12g	garlic
58g	gram flour	12g	salt
40g	sunflower oil		

Mix yogurt, gram flour, water, and spices. Add fried onions and potatoes and heat to thicken. Garnish with coriander.

Cooked weight 1030g

Nutrient content per 100g cooked weight

	Water	Protein	Fat	CHO	NSP	Energy	Energy
	g	g	g	g	g	kcals	kj
Average	66	5.0	12.7	10.4	1.4	170	705
Lower fat	70	4.7	4.9	15.2	1.8	120	505

90. PUNJABI KITCHADI (RICE AND LENTILS)

Average

135g	rice	26g	butter
135g	masoor dhal		
(salt, turmeric, garam masala)			

Cooked Weight 1084g

Lower Fat

100g	rice
185g	masoor dhal
(salt, turmeric, garam masala)	

Cooked Weight 2149g

Cook rice and beans in a lot of water with salt and spices (if used). When cooked stir thoroughly with added butter (if used)

Nutrient content per 100g cooked weight

	Water	Protein	Fat	CHO	NSP	Energy	Energy
	g	g	g	g	g	kcals	kj
Average	76	4.3	2.2	15.7	1.3	100	415
Low fat	84	2.7	0.2	12.3	0.4	60	255

Pulse dishes

91. GUJARATI KHICHADI

Average

218g mung   72g rice
110g ghee   (salt)

Cooked Weight 1280g

Lower Fat

155g rice   20g ghee
75g mung   (salt)

Cooked Weight 860g

Pressure-cook rice and mung in plenty of salted water. Stir in the ghee when cooked.

Nutrient content per 100g cooked weight

	Water	Protein	Fat	CHO	NSP	Energy	Energy
	g	g	g	g	g	kcals	kj
Average	71	5.0	8.8	12.4	1.7	150	615
Lower fat	72	3.5	2.6	19.7	1.0	110	465

92. ISMAILI KITCHADI

Average

184g polished white rice
78g mung dhal
12g salt
22g margarine

Cooked Weight 1300g

Lower Fat

196g basmati rice
142g masoor dhal
8g   salt

Cooked Weight 1060g

In a pressure cooker, cook rice and beans in a lot of water with salt. When cooked stir thoroughly with added margarine (if used).

Nutrient content per 100g cooked weight

	Water	Protein	Fat	CHO	NSP	Energy	Energy
	g	g	g	g	g	kcals	kj
Average	80	2.5	1.6	15.3	1.3	80	345
Lower fat	71	4.5	0.3	22.3	0.7	110	465

Rice and Cereal Dishes

Rice and Cereal dishes

93. PUNJABI MEAT PILAU

Average

940g	lamb	88g	corn oil
903g	rice	20g	garlic
225g	onions	20g	ginger
(salt, ground cumin, turmeric, garam masala)			

Cooked Weight 2840g

Blend onions, garlic and ginger and fry in oil. Add meat and spices and cook. Add potatoes. Separately, heat ghee and fry rice that has been pre-soaked. Add to the meat with boiling water and cook till the water is absorbed and the rice is done.

Nutrient content per 100g cooked weight

	Water	Protein	Fat	CHO	NSP	Energy	Energy
	g	g	g	g	g	kcals	kj
Average	50	7.8	15.4	28.5	0.2	280	1160

94. BENGALI MEAT PILAU/UKNI

Average

474g	rice	140g	vegetable oil
164g	onions	14g	salt
152g	lean lamb	8g	green chilli
140g	potatoes	1g	black pepper
98g	ghee	1g	bay leaf
40g	ginger	1g	cinnamon
12g	garlic	1g	cardamom

Cooked Weight 1646g

Blend onions, garlic and ginger and fry in oil. Add meat and spices and cook. Add potatoes. Separately heat ghee and fry rice that has been pre-soaked. Add to the meat with boiling water and cook till the water is absorbed and the rice is done.

Lower Fat

1445g	rice	25g	salt
895g	chicken	5g	cinnamon
565g	onions	2g	bay leaf
165g	butter ghee	2g	cardamom
20g	ginger	2g	cumin
15g	chillies	2g	turmeric
10g	garlic		

Cooked weight 3650g

Cook chicken, onions and salt without fat. Add garlic and ginger paste. Add ghee, cinnamon, bay leaf and cardamom. Separately fry onions and add rice when onions are brown. Add to chicken mixture with boiling water, simmer and cook till the water is absorbed and rice is done.

Nutrient content per 100g cooked weight

	Water	Protein	Fat	CHO	NSP	Energy	Energy
	g	g	g	g	g	kcals	kj
Average	55	4.5	13.6	25.6	0.4	245	1015
Lower fat	51	8.2	5.8	33.0	0.4	220	920

Rice and Cereal dishes

95. ISMAILI MEAT PILAU/UKNI (LAMB)

Average

438g	lamb meat
300g	basmati rice
275g	potatoes
82g	chopped onions
58g	sunflower oil
14g	garlic paste
14g	ginger paste

16g	fried onions
15g	salt
5g	cumin
4g	beef stock cube
3g	garam masala
2g	green chillies

Cooked Weight 1795g

Lower Fat

470g	potatoes
444g	lean lamb
420g	basmati rice
120g	tinned tomatoes
80g	onions
60g	sunflower oil

25g	fresh coriander
24g	fresh garlic
21g	ginger
6g	salt
6g	whole cumin
5g	chillies
4g	garam masala

Cooked Weight 2140g

Fry onions until soft then add spices. Add meat, tomatoes and potatoes. Add rice which has been previously soaked, washed and drained. Add water and bring to boil. Lower heat and simmer covered until dish is cooked.

Nutrient content per 100g cooked weight

	Water	Protein	Fat	CHO	NSP	Energy	Energy
	g	g	g	g	g	kcals	kj
Average	68	6.4	8.1	16.8	0.4	165	685
Lower fat	66	6.4	5.3	20.0	0.6	150	625

96. PAKISTANI MEAT PILAU

Average

594g	lamb
478g	rice
192g	onions
110g	corn oil
12g	salt

4g	cumin seeds
4g	garam masala
1g	cinnamon
1g	cloves

Cooked Weight 1990g

Lower Fat

748g	basmati rice
662g	lean lamb
354g	onions
150g	corn oil
122g	tomatoes
16g	garlic

12g	salt
2g	chilli powder
2g	garam masala
2g	ground cumin
2g	green chillies
2g	turmeric

Cooked Weight 3774g

Boil meat in water with salt, ginger, garlic, cinnamon, and cloves to make stock. Fry onions with cumin, garam masala and meat stock, bring to a boil. Soak rice for a short while and add to stock. Simmer till rice is done.

Nutrient content per 100g cooked weight

	Water	Protein	Fat	CHO	NSP	Energy	Energy
	g	g	g	g	g	kcals	kj
Average	55	7.0	16.1	20.0	0.3	255	1050
Lower fat	69	6.5	6.9	16.8	0.3	155	650

Rice and Cereal dishes

97. PUNJABI CHICKEN BIRYANI

Average

1000g rice	175g corn oil
840g chicken	15g garlic
195g onions	10g ginger
(salt, ground cumin, turmeric and garammasala)	

Cooked Weight 3440g

Lower Fat

2040g chicken legs	100g sunflower oil
1000g rice	20g garlic
225g plain yogurt	15g ginger
(salt, ground cumin, turmeric and garam masala)	

Cooked Weight 5080g

Boil meat in water with salt, ginger, garlic to make stock. Fry onions with cumin, turmeric and garam masala and add to meat and stock; bring to a boil, then add pre-soaked rice and simmer till rice is done. (If yogurt is used method as in no. 99)

Nutrient content per 100g cooked weight

	Water	Protein	Fat	CHO	NSP	Energy	Energy
	g	g	g	g	g	kcals	kj
Average	62	7.3	6.3	23.7	0.2	180	760
Lower fat	70	7.5	3.6	17.5	0.2	130	555

98. ISMAILI CHICKEN PILAU /UKNI

1035g chicken	20g garlic
826g basmati rice-	36g salt
394g potatoes	32g fresh coriander
152g onions	8g chillies
136g tinned tomatoes	4g garam masala
118g sunflower oil	

Cooked Weight 4300g

Cook meat in the pressure cooker with salt and garam masala. Fry onions and spices. Add meat and potatoes. Add stock. Add rice which has been previously soaked, washed and drained. Once boiled, lower the heat cover and simmer till water is absorbed.

Nutrient content per 100g cooked weight

	Water	Protein	Fat	CHO	NSP	Energy	Energy
		g	g	g	g	kcals	kj
Average	68	7.7	4.0	19.0	11.3	145	600

Rice and Cereal dishes

99. ISMAILI BIRYANI (CHICKEN)

Average

1250g	chicken
650g	rice
200g	fried onions
100g	yogurt
100g	tomatoes
100g	coriander
1g	saffron

50g	tomato puree
30g	sunflower oil
10g	garlic
5g	chillies
5g	salt
5g	turmeric

Cooked Weight 2506g

Put yogurt, spices, tomatoes, tomato puree and oil in the saucepan and cook. Add chicken and cook till done. Boil rice separately, when cooked add saffron to colour. Make a layer of meat and rice and top with fried onions

Nutrient content per 100g cooked weight

	Water	Protein	Fat	CHO	NSP	Energy	Energy
	g	g	g	g	g	kcals	kj
Average	58	12.8	4.5	22.7	0.5	185	770

100. PUNJABI PEAS PILAU

Average

400g	rice
370g	peas
96g	ghee

75g	onions
6g	chilli
	(salt, cumin seeds)

Cooked Weight 1520g

Lower Fat

300g	rice
250g	frozen peas
	(salt, chilli, cumin seeds)

180g	onions
60g	corn oil

Cooked Weight 1400g

Fry cumin seeds in oil, add onions, stir and fry. Add remaining ingredients, stir well to coat with fat. Then add water, bring to boil, cover and cook until water is absorbed.

Nutrient content per 100g cooked weight

	Water	Protein	Fat	CHO	NSP	Energy	Energy
	g	g	g	g	g	kcals	kj
Average	63	3.7	6.8	24.2	1.4	175	725
Lower fat	72	2.6	4.7	21.3	1.2	130	545

123

Rice and Cereal dishes

101. PUNJABI MIXED VEGETABLE PILAU

Average

340g	mixed vegetables	102g	butter
326g	rice	55g	onions
(salt, garlic, ginger, chilli, ground cumin, garam masala,			

Cooked Weight 1175g

Lower Fat

705g	rice	105g	onions
205g	mixed vegetables	90g	oil
(salt, garlic , ginger, chilli, ground cumin, garam masala)			

Cooked Weight 1900g

Fry onions. Add spices and all the ingredients except the rice. Cook till vegetables are slightly soft. Add rice and water. Bring to a boil. Simmer till done.

Nutrient content per 100g cooked weight

	Water	Protein	Fat	CHO	NSP	Energy	Energy
	g	g	g	g	g	kcals	kj
Average	62	3.3	7.5	25.0	1.3	180	755
Lower fat	59	2.5	4.9	31.3	0.7	170	725

102. PAKISTANI VEGETABLE PILAU

Average

804g	basmati ricé	11g	salt
380g	frozen peas	2g	chilli powder
80g	onions	2g	garlic
50g	vegetable oil	1g	ginger

Cooked Weight 1330g

Lower Fat

414g	basmati rice	26g	sunflower oil
152g	potatoes	8g	salt
84g	peas	2g	cumin
80g	carrots	1g	garlic
70g	onions	1g	garlic

Cooked Weight 1743g

Fry onions. Add spices and all the ingredients except the rice. Cook till vegetables are slightly soft. Add rice and water. Bring to a boil. Simmer till done.

Nutrient content per 100g cooked weight

	Water	Protein	Fat	CHO	NSP	Energy	Energy
	g	g	g	g	g	kcals	kj
Average	55	4.3	3.0	35.4	1.3	185	780
Lower fat	62	2.3	1.8	21.5	0.7	110	460

Rice dishes

103. ISMAILI RICE

Average

368g basmat rice
60g   sunflower oil
12g   salt

Cooked Weight 1440g

Heat oil. Add water and bring to boil. Add washed, drained rice and bring back to boil. Lower heat and cook until water is absorbed and rice is cooked.

Lower Fat

304g basmat rice
8g   salt

Cooked Weight 826g

Boil water. Add salt and rice. When rice is cooked drain off water and put in heated oven for rice to dry out.

Nutrient content per 100g cooked weight

	Water	Protein	Fat	CHO	NSP	Energy	Energy
	g	g	g	g	g	kcals	kj
Average	72	1.9	4.3	20.4	0.1	130	540
Lower fat	67	2.4	0.4	32.0	0.2	130	540

104. BENGALI RICE PITTA

Average

200g ground rice
1g   salt

Cooked weight 708g

In boiling, salted water add rice flour and cook until the mixture is solid and sticky. Put the mixture on a flat surface and knead. Make into sausage shaped balls. Steam for 15-20 minutes

Nutrient content per 100g cooked weight

	Water	Protein	Fat	CHO	NSP	Energy	Energy
		g	g	g	g	kcals	kj
Average	75	1.8	0.2	22.6	0.6	105	440

125

Rice and Cereal dishes

105. PUNJABI PARATHAS

Average

158g	flour
15g	butter ghee
Water	

Cooked Weight 255g (2 parathas)

Lower Fat

155g	flour
10g	butter
Water	(salt)

Mix butter into the flour and salt. Add sufficient water, gathering dough into a ball. The dough should be soft. Knead for 10 minutes and set aside in a covered bowl for half an hour. Fry on both sides on a heated griddle.

Cooked Weight 252g (2 parathas)

Nutrient content per 100g cooked weight

	Water	Protein	Fat	CHO	NSP	Energy	Energy
	g	g	g	g	g	kcals	kj
Average	39	6.1	6.2	48.5	1.9	260	1090
Lower fat	41	6.1	3.6	47.8	1.9	235	1000

106. PAKISTANI PARATHA

Average

688g	white chapati flour
140g	vegetable oil
8g	salt
Water	

Cooked Weight 1176g

Add water to flour and salt to make dough. Roll balls of dough and spread oil around and fold in oil into ball again. Roll out again and fry on both sides.

Nutrient content per 100g cooked weight

	Water	Protein	Fat	CHO	NSP	Energy	Energy
		g	g	g	g	kcals	kj
Average	36	5.7	12.2	45.4	1.9	305	1285

Rice dishes

107. PUNJABI METHI PARATHAS

Average

390g wholemeal flour 15g corn oil
145g methi   15g salt
(green chilli, ground coriander)

Cooked Weight 715g

Lower Fat

630g wholemeal flour 70g onions
165g methi
(salt, green chilli, ground coriander)

Cooked Weight 1115g

Make parathas as no 106. Cook spinach, drain well and puree. Fry spices, add spinach and salt and mix. Use to stuff parathas. (Lower fat version - cook spinach and chopped onions together before blending and re-cooking with spices and salt)

Nutrient content per 100g cooked weight

	Water	Protein	Fat	CHO	NSP	Energy	Energy
		g	g	g	g	kcals	kj
Average	46	7.2	2.8	41.2	5.4	210	880
Lower fat	47	7.3	0.7	42.9	4.3	195	830

108. BENGALI PARATHAS

Average

65g white chapati flour
16g vegetable oil
16g ghee or butter
1g   salt
Water to mix

Cooked Weight 140g, 3 portions

Lower Fat

158g white chapati flour
16g   oil
26g   ghee or butter
1g   salt
Water to mix

Cooked Weight 254g, 6 portions

Mix all the ingredients with hot water and knead. Divide into portions. Roll out and fry in ghee or butter.

Nutrient content per 100g cooked weight

	Water	Protein	Fat	CHO	NSP	Energy	Energy
		g	g	g	g	kcals	kj
Average	36	4.6	23	36.0	1.4	360	1505
Lower fat	30	6.1	16.8	48.2	1.9	355	1490

Rice dishes

109. PAKISTANI ROTI

Average

1058g wholewheat chapati flour
Water

Cooked Weight 1478g

Knead flour with warm water until firm dough. Roll out into round chapatis and cook.

Nutrient content per 100g cooked weight

	Water g	Protein g	Fat g	CHO g	NSP g	Energy kcals	Energy kj
Average	37	8.2	0.9	53	4.5	240	1030

110. ISMAILI ROTI/ROTLI/CHAPATI

Average

600g   wholemeal chapati flour
50g   sunflower oil
35g   margarine
2g   salt

Cooked Weight 950g

Mix oil, flour and salt with enough water to make a dough. Roll out chapatis and cook on stove. Spread with margarine.

Nutrient content per 100g cooked weight

	Water g	Protein g	Fat g	CHO g	NSP g	Energy kcals	Energy kj
Average	24	8.6	10.9	55.2	4.8	340	1430

Rice dishes

111. BENGALI CHAPATI

Average

235g white chapati flour
      Water to mix

Cooked Weigh: 325g

Knead the dough with warm water. Divide into three portions. Roll out and heat.

Nutrient content per 100g cooked weight

	Water g	Protein g	Fat g	CHO g	NSP g	Energy kcals	Energy kj
Average	36	7.1	0.4	56	2.2	240	1025

112. ISMAILI DHOKRA

Average

392g buttermilk
226g semolina
28g   sunflower oil
12g   garlic powder
10g   ginger powder

Cooked Weight 770g

Mix all the ingredients in a large bowl. Add the sachet of Eno and transfer to a greased tin. Steam for 15 minutes.

Low Fat

426g low fat natural yogurt
378g semolina
48g   gram flour
38g   skinless mung dhal
36g   onions
33g   citric acid
14g   crushed ginger
14g   crushed garlic
6g   cumin

14g   coriander paste
8g   chilli paste
2g   salt
1 sachet liver salts, eg. Eno

fresh coriander
22g   sunflower oil
20g   coriander paste
20g   chilli paste
20g   fenugreek
18g   liver salts, eg. Eno
8g   salt
3g   turmeric

Cooked Weight 1832g

Soak all the ingredients for 3-4 hours apart from onions, coriander, chillies and fenugreek. Add onions, coriander, chillies and fenugreek and divide the mixture into three portions. Add 6g of Eno into each portion and mix well. Steam for 12-15 minutes per portion.

Nutrient content per 100g cooked weight

	Water g	Protein g	Fat g	CHO g	NSP g	Energy kcals	Energy kj
Average	63	5.3	4.5	26.9	0.8	160	685
Low fat	68	5.2	2.4	20.1	0.8	115	485

Meat Dishes

Meat dishes

113. PUNJABI LAMB CURRY

Average

374g	lamb shoulder
265g	onions
250g	tinned tomatoes

100g	vegetable oil
16g	ginger
10g	garlic

(salt, chilli, ground turmeric, cumin)

Cooked Weight 1200g

Lower Fat

1660g	lamb
397g	tinned tomatoes
175g	onions

25g	butter
5g	chillies

(salt, chilli, garlic, ginger, ground turmeric, cumin)

Cooked Weight 1550g

Heat oil. Add onions, garlic, green chilli and ginger. Add meat and water and simmer till meat is tender. Add tomatoes and cook to desired consistency.

Nutrient content per 100g cooked weight

	Water g	Protein g	Fat g	CHO g	NSP g	Energy kcals	Energy kj
Average	71	5.9	18.4	3.1	0.6	200	835
Lower fat	64	22.8	10.9	1.7	0.4	195	820

114. PUNJABI LAMB AND POTATO CURRY

Average

1180g	lamb
420g	potatoes
204g	onions

13g	chillies
12g	garlic
11g	ginger

(salt, ground turmeric, cumin)

Cooked Weight 1520g

Heat oil. Add onions, garlic, green chilli and ginger. Add meat and water and simmer till meat is tender. Add tomatoes and potatoes cook to desired consistency.

Nutrient content per 100g cooked weight

	Water g	Protein g	Fat g	CHO g	NSP g	Energy kcals	Energy kj
Average	63	14.8	14.6	6.3	0.6	215	895

Meat dishes

115. PUNJABI MUTTON CURRY

Average

954g	mutton	16g	ginger
290g	onions	13g	garlic
31g	ghee	5g	chilli
(salt, ground turmeric, cumin)			

Cooked Weight 1460g

Lower Fat

540g	mutton	80g	ghee
250g	onions	25g	chillies
(salt, ground turmeric, cumin)			

Cooked Weight 1480g

Heat oil, add onions, garlic, green chilli and ginger. Add meat and water and simmer till meat is tender and curry is the desired consistency.

Nutrient content per 100g cooked weight

	Water	Protein	Fat	CHO	NSP	Energy	Energy
		g	g	g	g	kcals	kj
Average	72	6.8	19	1.5	0.3	205	850
Lower fat	76	13.9	7.9	1.9	0.3	135	560

116. PUNJABI LAMB CHOPS

Average

1840g	lamb chops	35g	garlic
230g	tomatoes	35g	ginger
205g	onions	20g	chilli
100g	sunflower oil		
(salt, ground turmeric, cumin, garam masala)			

Cooked Weight 2100g

Lower Fat

1000g	lamb chops	33g	ghee
344g	fresh tomatoes	8g	garlic
170g	onions		
(salt, ground turmeric, cumin, garam masala)			

Cooked Weight 2000g

Heat oil add onions, garlic, green chilli and ginger. Add meat and water and simmer till meat is tender. Add tomatoes and potatoes cook to desired consistency.

Nutrient content per 100g cooked weight

	Water	Protein	Fat	CHO	NSP	Energy	Energy
		g	g	g	g	kcals	kj
Average	48	13.2	35.9	1.6	0.3	380	1585
Lower fat	68	7.6	22.4	1.3	0.3	235	975

Meat dishes

117. ISMAILI MEAT CURRY (LAMB)

Average

626g	lamb meat	4g	coriander powder
150g	tinned tomatoes	4g	cumin powder
60g	fried onions	8g	green chillies
34g	mixed vegetable oil	1g	turmeric
24g	fresh garlic	1g	garam masala
18g	fresh ginger		
6g	salt		

Cooked Weight 1115g

Lower Fat (using beef)

494g	lean beef	10g	ginger
472g	potatoes	9g	cumin powder
264g	tinned tomatoes	9g	coriander powder
82g	fried onions	2g	garam masala
15g	salt		
10g	garlic		

Cooked Weight 2175g

Cook the meat in pressure cooker. Fry tomatoes, spices and cooked meat. Add water and cook till done.

Lower fat - cook the meat in pressure cooker. Add tomatoes, spices and water and cook till done.

Nutrient content per 100g cooked weight

	Water	Protein	Fat	CHO	NSP	Energy	Energy
	g	g	g	g	g	kcals	kj
Average	75	12.3	8.8	1.8	0.4	135	555
Lower fat	85	5.5	1.6	4.9	0.5	55	230

118. PAKISTANI LAMB CURRY

Average

330g	lamb	6g	garlic
120g	tomatoes	5g	salt
80g	onions	4g	fresh coriander
57g	corn oil	3g	coriander powder
25g	yogurt	3g	cumin powder
25g	ginger	2g	turmeric
7g	green chillies		

Cooked Weight 672g

Lower Fat

1048g	lamb chops	22g	ginger
204g	tomatoes	18g	garlic
188g	onions	14g	salt
86g	ghee	6g	chilli powder
4g	turmeric	2g	garam masala

Cooked Weight 1452g

Brown onions. Add spices and tomatoes. Add meat and water. Cook until done. Garnish with coriander

Lower fat - put all the ingredients in a pressure cooker with water and boil. When meat is cooked, add ghee and more water and cook till done.

Nutrient content per 100g cooked weight

	Water	Protein	Fat	CHO	NSP	Energy	Energy
	g	g	g	g	g	kcals	kj
Average	60	9.1	25.9	2.6	0.4	275	1140
Lower fat	67	15.5	12.4	1.9	0.3	180	755

134

119. BENGALI LAMB CURRY

Average

1390g	lean lamb	17g	fresh coriander
450g	onions	3g	coriander powder
195g	corn oil	2g	cinnamon
35g	garlic	2g	cardamom
30g	salt	1g	cloves
20g	curry powder	1g	bay leaf
15g	ginger	1g	turmeric

Cooked Weight 1890g

Lower Fat

909g	lean lamb	26g	salt
206g	onions	17g	curry powder
47g	vegetable oil	10g	garam masala
24g	ginger	10g	coriander powder
24g	garlic		

Cooked Weight 1804g

Fry spices, garlic and ginger. Add meat, onions and fry. Add water and cook till meat is tender.

Nutrient content per 100g cooked weight

	Water	Protein	Fat	CHO	NSP	Energy	Energy
	g	g	g	g	g	kcals	kj
Average	60	16.1	17.4	2.8	0.4	230	955
Lower fat	76	11.3	7.4	2.3	0.6	120	500

120. PUNJABI LAMB KEEMA (MINCED)

Average

1500g	lamb	50g	garlic
500g	onions	40g	chilli
140g	corn oil	30g	ginger
(salt, ground coriander, cumin, turmeric)			

Cooked Weight 2218g

Lower Fat

475g	minced lamb	20g	chillies
400g	tomatoes	5g	ghee
130g	onions		
(salt, ground coriander, cumin, turmeric)			

Cooked Weight 1030g

Fry onions with garlic and ginger till brown. Add meat and cook. Add tomatoes and spices. Cook till all liquid disappears and oil reappears. Add water and salt and cook until meat is cooked through.

Nutrient content per 100g cooked weight

	Water	Protein	Fat	CHO	NSP	Energy	Energy
	g	g	g	g	g	kcals	kj
Average	55	11.9	30.0	2.5	0.5	330	1355
Lower fat	72	8.3	16.5	2.4	0.5	190	790

121. PUNJABI MATUR KEEMA (LAMB AND PEAS)

Average

1355g	minced lamb	145g	peas
812g	onions	28g	chilli
400g	tinned tomatoes	25g	garlic
254g	margarine	12g	ginger

(Salt, ground coriander, cumin, turmeric, fresh coriander, lemon juice)

Cooked Weight 2700g

Lower Fat

1380g	minced lamb	145g	tomatoes
700g	onions	55g	butter
370g	frozen peas	35g	chillies

(salt, garlic, ginger, ground coriander, cumin, turmeric, fresh coriander, lemon juice)

Cooked Weight 2530g

Fry onions till lightly brown, add garlic, mince, ginger, chillies and spices. Stir to break up meat and add water. Bring to the boil, simmer till meat is cooked. Add peas, fresh coriander, salt and lemon juice and cook till peas are tender.

Nutrient content per 100g cooked weight

	Water	Protein	Fat	CHO	NSP	Energy	Energy
	g	g	g	g	g	kcals	kj
Average	67	10.0	17.3	3.8	0.4	210	870
Lower fat	72	11.1	12.2	3.9	1.2	165	700

122. ISMAILI LAMB KEEMA (MINCED MEAT CURRY)

Average

444g	lamb lean mince	10g	minced ginger
397g	tinned tomatoes	2g	chillies
68g	onions	2g	salt
10g	sunflower oil	1g	cumin powder
12g	minced garlic	1g	coriander powder
10g	minced ginger		

Cooked Weight 1202g

Lower Fat

466g	lean beef mince	24g	fried onions
560g	potatoes	14g	garlic
198g	fresh tomatoes	6g	salt
100g	tomato puree	4g	lemon juice
48g	yogurt	2g	garam masala
46g	fresh coriander	2g	coriander powder
20g	fresh coriander(garnish)	1g	cinnamon
24g	margarine	1g	cloves

Cooked Weight 1726g

Fry onions till brown. Add meat and cook. Add tomatoes and spices. Cook till all liquid disappears and oil reappears. Add water and salt. Garnish with fresh coriander if used.

Nutrient content per 100g cooked weight

	Water	Protein	Fat	CHO	NSP	Energy	Energy
	g	g	g	g	g	kcals	kj
Average	76	6.8	13.7	2.0	0.6	160	650
Lower fat	78	6.5	7.5	0.8	0.4	105	445

Meta dishes

123. PAKISTANI LAMB KEEMA (MINCE MEAT)

Average

270g	minced lamb	12g	garlic
242g	onions	12g	salt
130g	sunflower oil	8g	coriander
84g	tinned tomatoes	4g	chilli powder
14g	ginger	2g	turmeric

Cooked Weight 778g

Lower Fat

1030g	minced lamb	3g	chilli powder
338g	onions	3g	cumin
64g	butter ghee	2g	dry coriander
60g	tinned tomatoes	2g	salt
16g	ginger	2g	turmeric
16g	garlic	1g	garam masala
5g	fresh coriander		

Cooked Weight 2190g

Brown meat. Add oil, spices, tomatoes, ginger, garlic, and onions with water. Cook till done. Garnish with coriander and/or garam masala.

Nutrient content per 100g cooked weight

	Water	Protein	Fat	CHO	NSP	Energy	Energy
	g	g	g	g	g	kcals	kj
Average	60	6.3	26.8	3.2	0.6	275	1135
Lower fat	80	10.2	7.3	1.6	0.3	110	460

124. PAKISTANI MATAR KEEMA (MINCED MEAT AND PEAS)

Average

1014g	minced lamb	16g	ginger
358g	onions	12g	turmeric
266g	peas	6g	chilli powder
214g	tinned tomatoes	6g	dry coriander
50g	vegetable ghee	6g	salt
18g	garlic	3g	fresh coriander

Cooked Weight 1979g

Lower Fat

405g	peas	14g	salt
320g	minced lamb (lean)	12g	ginger
180g	onions	8g	chilli powder
60g	corn oil	8g	dry coriander
80	tinned tomatoes	3g	turmeric
20g	garlic		

Cooked Weight 1140g

Brown meat. Add oil or ghee, spices, tomatoes, ginger, garlic, and onions with water. Add peas and cook till done. Garnish with coriander if used.

Nutrient content per 100g cooked weight

	Water	Protein	Fat	CHO	NSP	Energy	Energy
	g	g	g	g	g	kcals	kj
Average	60	14.4	16.9	5.1	1.4	230	945
Lower fat	69	8.0	10.3	5.4	2.2	140	585

125. PAKISTANI ALOO KEEMA (POTATO AND MINCED BEEF)

Average

454g	minced beef	
310g	potatoes	
144g	onions	
108g	tomatoes	
62g	sunflower oil	
24g	ginger	

20g	garlic
4g	ground coriander
4g	salt
2g	chilli powder
1g	turmeric

Cooked Weight 833g

Brown onions in oil. Add spices, tomatoes and meat. Add potatoes with water. Cook till done.

Nutrient content per 100g cooked weight

	Water g	Protein g	Fat g	CHO g	NSP g	Energy kcals	Energy kj
Average	61	11.4	15.9	9.9	1.1	225	925

126. BENGALI LAMB KEEMA

Average

1130g	lamb mince	
370g	onions	
80g	vegetable oil	
35g	salt	
25g	fresh coriander	
15g	ginger	

15g	curry powder
10g	garlic
10g	garam masala
2g	cumin
2g	coriander
1g	turmeric

Cooked Weight 1635g

Fry onions, ginger and garlic. Add mince and garam masala. Cook for a while and add the rest of the ingredients plus water. Cook till the mince is done.

Nutrient content per 100g cooked weight

	Water g	Protein g	Fat g	CHO g	NSP g	Energy kcals	Energy kj
Average	51	12.3	29.1	3.1	0.6	320	1325

Meat dishes

127. PUNJABI LAMB KEBAB

Average

226g	lamb	5g	chillies
90g	onions	4g	garlic
15g	coriander		

(salt, paprika pepper, cumin seeds, fresh mint, fresh parsley)

Cooked Weight 270g

Mix all the ingredients together. Shape tablespoons of the mixture around one end of a skewer to form into sausage shapes, and grill.

Nutrient content per 100g cooked weight

	Water	Protein	Fat	CHO	NSP	Energy	Energy
	g	g	g	g	g	kcals	kj
Average	64	15.7	15.8	3.2	0.5	215	895

128. PAKISTANI ALOO GOSHT

Average

692g	leg lamb	20g	ginger
484g	onions	20g	dry coriander
398g	potatoes	16g	salt
100g	tomatoes	8g	garam masala
72g	sunflower oil	5g	chilli powder
34g	fresh coriander	5g	turmeric
20g	garlic		

Cooked Weight 1676g

Lower Fat

333g	lean lamb	16g	ginger
220g	onions	7g	salt
170g	potatoes	6g	green chillies
164g	tomatoes	2g	garlic
20g	sunflower oil		

Cooked Weight 1252g

Fry onions. Add meat and spices with water. Add potatoes and tomatoes. Simmer till done

Nutrient content per 100g cooked weight

	Water	Protein	Fat	CHO	NSP	Energy	Energy
	g	g	g	g	g	kcals	kj
Average	68	8.9	12.4	7.6	0.8	175	725
Lower fat	84	6.2	4.0	4.4	0.5	80	335

Meat dishes

129. PAKISTANI KOFTA (MEAT BALLS)

Average

Meat Balls
555g minced meat
17g garlic
14g ginger
10g salt

Sauce
150g sunflower oil
200g onions
83g tomatoes
10g ground coriander
5g salt
5g chilli powder
2g turmeric

Cooked Weight 1051g

Lower Fat

568g minced lamb
176g onions
8g salt
1g chilli powder
1g cumin seeds
1g poppy seeds

150g onions
108g yogurt
106g tomatoes
62g ghee
8g garlic
6g salt
2g garam masala
1g chilli powder

Cooked Weight 2300g

Mix ingredients for meat balls in a food processor and shape into balls. Put ingredients for sauce in a pan and heat in ghee. Add water and meatballs and bring to a boil. Add yogurt or oil if used and cook till ghee separates from curry.

Nutrient content per 100g cooked weight

	Water	Protein	Fat	CHO	NSP	Energy	Energy
	g	g	g	g	g	kcals	kj
Average	60	10.2	24.3	2.5	0.4	270	1110
Lower fat	86	5.7	5.0	1.7	0.3	75	310

130. PAKISTANI GOSHT PALAK (MEAT AND SPINACH)

Average

805g lean lamb
727g tinned spinach
320g onions
135g vegetable oil
102g tinned tomatoes
31g coriander powder

11g green chillies
10g salt
4g chilli powder
2g garlic
2g ginger
2g turmeric

Cooked Weight 1833g

Fry onions and spices. Add meat. Add spinach and chillies. Cook till done.

Nutrient content per 100g cooked weight

	Water	Protein	Fat	CHO	NSP	Energy	Energy
	g	g	g	g	g	kcals	kj
Average	75	9.5	9.4	2.0	0.9	125	520

140

Meat dishes

131. PUNJABI CHICKEN CURRY

Average

2620g	chicken
560g	onions
430g	tomatoes
(salt, ground turmeric)	

120g	corn oil
50g	ginger
45g	garlic

Cooked Weight 4114g

Lower Fat

3600g	chicken
1090g	tinned tomatoes
244g	fresh tomatoes
70g	chillies
(salt, ground turmeric)	

50g	cumin
40g	corn oil
30g	garlic
30g	ginger

Cooked Weight 4600g

Fry onions, garlic, ginger and chicken. Add tomatoes, spices, lemon and water. Cook till the chicken is tender.

Nutrient content per 100g cooked weight

	Water	Protein	Fat	CHO	NSP	Energy	Energy
	g	g	g	g	g	kcals	kj
Average	78	13.4	5.7	1.7	0.3	110	465
Lower fat	79	14.5	3.9	1.2	0.3	100	420

132. PUNJABI CHICKEN CURRY WITH YOGURT

Average

1340g	chicken
424g	tinned tomatoes
230g	oil
186g	onions
92g	fresh tomatoes
(salt, ground turmeric)	

67g	yogurt
22g	tomato puree
11g	garlic
7g	ginger
6g	chilli

Cooked Weight 2230g

Lower Fat

1540g	chicken
198g	onions
96g	yogurt
salt, chilli, garlic, ground turmeric)	

88g	corn oil
66g	tomatoes
18g	ginger

Cooked Weight 1760g

Place garlic, ginger, tomato puree, spices, yogurt and salt in a bowl, mix well and put in chicken pieces. Leave for at least 4 hours. Fry onions, add tomatoes, chicken and marinade and bring to simmering point and cook till chicken is tender.

Nutrient content per 100g cooked weight

	Water	Protein	Fat	CHO	NSP	Energy	Energy
	g	g	g	g	g	kcals	kj
Average	71	12.9	13.0	1.8	0.3	175	730
Lower fat	65	22.1	9.8	1.5	0.2	180	760

Meat dishes

133. PAKISTANI CHICKEN CURRY

Average

1260g	chicken
780g	tinned tomatoes
480g	onions
455g	corn oil
150g	ginger
60g	garlic
48g	fresh coriander
30g	cumin powder
25g	coriander powder
12g	turmeric

Cooked Weight 3340g

Lower Fat

1804g	chicken
416g	onions
60g	tinned tomatoes
56g	ghee
14g	chilli powder
12g	salt
10g	ginger
8g	coriander powder
6g	garlic
2g	fresh coriander
2g	turmeric
1g	cumin powder

Cooked Weight 3178g

Brown onions. Add tomatoes and spices. Add chicken and water. Cook till done. Garnish with fresh coriander.

Nutrient content per 100g cooked weight

	Water	Protein	Fat	CHO	NSP	Energy	Energy
	g	g	g	g	g	kcals	kj
Average	69	8.7	15.7	2.6	0.4	180	750
Lower fat	80	12.0	4.3	1.3	0.2	90	380

134. BENGALI CHICKEN CURRY

Average

1660g	chicken
530g	onions
170g	corn oil
120g	lemon juice
35g	garlic
25g	ginger
25g	salt
20g	curry powder
5g	coriander
3g	cinnamon
2g	cardamom
2g	cloves
2g	turmeric
1g	bay leaf

Cooked Weight 2350g

Lower Fat

974g	chicken
432g	onions
54g	vegetable oil
34g	fresh coriander
42g	garlic
18g	salt
16g	curry powder
8g	chilli powder

Cooked Weight 1482g

Fry onions, garlic, ginger and chicken. Add spices, lemon juice and water. Cook till the chicken is tender. Garnish with coriander.

Nutrient content per 100g cooked weight

	Water	Protein	Fat	CHO	NSP	Energy	Energy
	g	g	g	g	g	kcals	kj
Average	68	15.1	10.5	2.6	0.6	165	680
Lower fat	72	14.3	6.8	3.1	0.6	130	545

Meat dishes

135. BENGALI CHICKEN BHUNA

Average

1210g	chicken	26g	fresh coriander
238g	onions	16g	chilli powder
78g	sunflower oil	10g	salt
11g	garlic	6g	turmeric
11g	ginger	6g	coriander powder
10g	salt	6g	curry powder
6g	cumin powder	1g	fenugreek seeds
1g	bay leaf		

Cooked Weight 1326g

Fry garlic, ginger, bay leaf and fenugreek. Add onions, chicken and salt and cook. Add spices and coriander.

Nutrient content per 100g cooked weight

	Water	Protein	Fat	CHO	NSP	Energy	Energy
	g	g	g	g	g	kcals	kj
Average	65	19.5	10.3	2.0	0.4	175	725

136. ISMAILI CHICKEN AND POTATO CURRY

Average

956g	chicken	7g	turmeric
478g	potatoes	5g	fresh coriander
234g	tinned tomatoes	5g	ginger paste
82g	onions	4g	coriander powder
64g	sunflower oil	3g	cumin powder
10g	salt	2g	garam masala
5g	garlic paste	2g	lemon juice

Cooked Weight 2077g

Lower Fat

1058g	chicken	8g	salt
348g	potatoes	1g	turmeric
280g	tinned tomatoes	1g	chilli powder
164g	onions	1g	cumin powder
60g	tomato puree	1g	coriander powder
38g	garlic	1g	garam masala
26g	ginger		

Cooked Weight 2028g

Fry onions, garlic, ginger and tomatoes. Add spices and tomato and fry. Add water and boil. Add chicken and cook till tender. Add garam masala.

Nutrient content per 100g cooked weight

	Water	Protein	Fat	CHO	NSP	Energy	Energy
	g	g	g	g	g	kcals	kj
Average	78	10.1	5.3	4.5	0.4	105	435
Lower fat	79	11.6	2.4	4.9	0.6	85	360

137. BENGALI CHICKEN AND POTATO CURRY

Average

546g	chicken
118g	onions
160g	potatoes
68g	corn oil
5g	ginger
3g	garlic
4g	red chillies

6g	fresh coriander
4g	coriander powder
4g	salt
4g	cumin
1g	turmeric

Cooked Weight 970g

Fry onions, garlic and ginger. Add chicken and salt cook for a while. Add spices and water with potatoes and boil. Garnish with coriander.

Nutrient content per 100g cooked weight

	Water	Protein	Fat	CHO	NSP	Energy	Energy
		g	g	g	g	kcals	kj
Average	72	12.3	9.6	4.1	0.4	150	625

138. PAKISTANI ROAST CHICKEN

Average

1092g	chicken
26g	plain yogurt
6g	chilli powder
6g	garlic

6g	ginger
6g	salt
1g	black pepper powder

Cooked Weight 958g

Marinate chicken in masalas (spices in yogurt) for a few hours. Preheat oven to gas mark 6. Cook until done. Sprinkle with black pepper before serving.

Nutrient content per 100g cooked weight

	Water	Protein	Fat	CHO	NSP	Energy	Energy
		g	g	g	g	kcals	kj
Average	69	23.6	5.1	0.3	0	140	590

Egg and Cheese Dishes

Egg and Cheese dishes

139. PUNJABI MATAR PANEER (CURD CHEESE)

Average

710g	paneer
524g	onions
370g	frozen peas
238g	tinned tomatoes

150g	ghee
13g	fresh chillies
10g	fresh coriander
	(salt)

Cooked Weight 1350g

Lower Fat

330g	tomatoes
235g	peas
220g	onions
170g	paneer

25g	garlic
25g	ghee
25g	ginger
20g	coriander
	(salt)

Cooked Weight 440g

Put onion and ginger (if used) in a blender with a little water, and blend to a paste. Fry paneer until brown, remove from pan and fry garlic and chillies (if used). Add contents of blender to pan, fry until brown then add ground spices. Add tomatoes, cook for 10 minutes and then add paneer and peas and simmer until peas are cooked.

Nutrient content per 100g cooked weight

	Water	Protein	Fat	CHO	NSP	Energy	Energy
	g	g	g	g	g	kcals	kj
Average	46	14.9	24.6	9.6	2.1	320	1330
Lower fat	55	10.4	13.4	13.0	3.8	210	875

140. PUNJABI MATAR PANEER WITH POTATOES

Average

640g	potatoes
398g	tinned tomatoes
250g	peas
200g	paneer
172g	onions

100g	margarine
23g	ginger
18g	garlic
11g	chilli
5g	coriander

Cooked Weight 2382g

Dice and boil the potatoes. Put onion and ginger (if used) in a blender with a little water, and blend to a paste. Fry paneer until brown, remove from pan and fry garlic and chillies (if used). Add contents of blender to pan, fry until brown then add ground spices. Add tomatoes, cook for 10 minutes and then add paneer, potatoes and peas and simmer until peas are cooked.

Nutrient content per 100g cooked weight

	Water	Protein	Fat	CHO	NSP	Energy	Energy
	g	g	g	g	g	kcals	kj
Average	81	3.5	5.7	7.5	1.2	95	395

Egg and Cheese dishes

141. PUNJABI SPINACH (PALAK) PANEER

Average

916g	spinach	80g	butter
578g	paneer	78g	fresh methi
252g	onions	58g	ginger
250g	tinned tomatoes	18g	garlic
222g	sunflower oil		(salt)

Cooked Weight 2190g

Put onion and ginger in blender with a little water and blend to a paste. Fry paneer in oil and butter until brown. Remove paneer from pan and fry methi and garlic. Add contents of blender to pan, fry until brown and then add salt. Add tomatoes and spinach, cook for 15 minutes and then add paneer and cook for a further 10 minutes.

Nutrient content per 100g cooked weight

	Water	Protein	Fat	CHO	NSP	Energy	Energy
		g	g	g	g	kcals	kj
Average	64	8.1	20.1	4.1	1.2	230	935

142. BENGALI EGG CURRY

Average

8 large eggs		6g	coriander powder
466g	onions	4g	turmeric
112g	corn oil	4g	red chilli powder
16g	fresh coriander	4g	cumin powder
8g	salt	2g	curry powder
2g	bay leaf		

Cooked Weight 728g

Boil eggs. Fry onions and spices. Add eggs and cook for a few minutes.

Nutrient content per 100g cooked weight

	Water	Protein	Fat	CHO	NSP	Energy	Energy
		g	g	g	g	kcals	kj
Average	55	10.5	23.9	5.7	1.0	275	1140

Fish Dishes

Fish dishes

143. ISMAILI MASALA FISH

Average

252g	potatoes
208g	frozen coley
130g	tinned tomatoes
54g	fried onions
34g	lemon juice
32g	vegetable oil

16g	tomato puree
14g	fresh garlic
4g	salt
4g	chilli powder
2g	cumin
1g	coriander powder

Cooked Weight 506g

Fry fish in oil, then remove fish from pan. In same oil cook spices and tomatoes. Add fried onions and potatoes, and cook. Then add fish and heat through.

Nutrient content per 100g cooked weight

	Water	Protein	Fat	CHO	NSP	Energy	Energy
	g	g	g	g	g	kcals	kj
Average	67	8.7	8.4	11.3	1.2	150	630

144. BENGALI BAIM (BAAM/BAING) FISH AND POTATO

Average

338g	baim fish
148g	onions
298g	potatoes
92g	vegetable oil
20g	salt
26g	garlic
6g	green chillies

2g	curry powder
2g	coriander powder
2g	cumin powder
2g	chilli powder
2g	turmeric
1g	bay leaf
1g	fresh coriander

Cooked Weight 1320g

Fry onions and spices. Add water and potatoes and fish and boil. Garnish with coriander.

Lower Fat

340g	baim fish
218g	onions
414g	potatoes
74g	corn oil

16g	green chillies
10g	fresh coriander
8g	turmeric
8g	chilli powder

Cooked Weight 1360g

Boil onions in a little water. Add oil and spices and cook. Add fish and more water and cook. Garnish with fresh coriander.

Nutrient content per 100g cooked weight

	Water	Protein	Fat	CHO	NSP	Energy	Energy
	g	g	g	g	g	kcals	kj
Average	65	15.3	7.4	6.3	0.6	145	600
Lower fat	79	5.5	6.8	7.0	0.7	105	445

Fish dishes

145. BENGALI BOAL FISH

Average

668g	boal	12g	turmeric
290g	onions	12g	green chillies
90g	oil	4g	chilli powder
24g	salt	2g	cumin powder
30g	fresh coriander	2g	coriander powder

Cooked Weight 1230g

Lower Fat

830g	boal	6g	curry powder
170g	onions	4g	turmeric
45g	vegetable oil	4g	chilli powder
18g	salt	2g	cumin powder
6g	green chillies		

Cooked Weight 1500g

Fry onions and spices. Add fish, water and boil.

Nutrient content per 100g cooked weight

	Water	Protein	Fat	CHO	NSP	Energy	Energy
	g	g	g	g	g	kcals	kj
Average	72	8.9	8.8	2.0	0.4	120	500
Lower fat	78	8.8	4.7	1.0	0.3	80	335

146. BENGALI GARGOT (AYR) FISH

Average

476g	gargot fish	8g	chilli powder
80g	onions	2g	turmeric
70g	mixed vegetable oil	0.5g	coriander powder
24g	fresh coriander	0.5g	cumin powder
12g	salt		

Cooked Weight 1044g

Fry onions and spices. Add water and fish and cook. Garnish with coriander.

Nutrient content per 100g cooked weight

	Water	Protein	Fat	CHO	NSP	Energy	Energy
	g	g	g	g	g	kcals	kj
Average	80	7.8	7.7	0.7	0.1	100	420

147. BENGALI GOJAR SHUTKI (DRY) FISH

Average

76g	onions	2g	chilli powder
72g	dry gojar fish	2g	curry power
52g	mixed vegetable oil	1g	cumin
8g	salt	1g	turmeric

Cooked Weight 220g

Lower Fat

116g	dry gojar fish	10g	green chillies
112g	onions	7g	garlic
30g	sunflower oil	4g	curry powder
14g	salt	1g	cumin powder
1g	turmeric	1g	chilli powder

Cooked Weight 540g

Soak dry fish for a few hours to soften. Fry onions and spices. Add fish and water and boil.

Nutrient content per 100g cooked weight

	Water	Protein	Fat	CHO	NSP	Energy	Energy
	g	g	g	g	g	kcals	kj
Average	42	19	24.3	4.3	0.7	300	1240
Lower fat	72	12.5	5.9	2.9	0.5	110	450

148. BENGALI HIDOL SHUTKI (DRY) CHUTNEY

Average

255g	onions	12g	chilli powder
75g	dry hidol fish	10g	salt
30g	mixed vegetable oil		

Cooked Weight 330g

Fry onions. Separately fry fish. Put onions and fish in blender with spices and salt and blend to a paste, adding little water.

Lower Fat

40g	dry hidol fish	5g	chilli powder
40g	fresh garlic	2g	salt

Cooked Weight 100g

Char fish in hot pan without any oil. Grind charred fish with garlic, salt and chillies and little water to a smooth paste.

Nutrient content per 100g cooked weight

	Water	Protein	Fat	CHO	NSP	Energy	Energy
	g	g	g	g	g	kcals	kj
Average	63	7.3	14.6	6.2	1.1	170	700
Lower fat	53	15.1	9.8	7.1	1.8	150	635

Fish dishes

149. BENGALI ILLISH (HILSHA) FISH

Average

786g	illish fish	6g	coriander powder
208g	onions	6g	curry powder
102g	mix vegetable oil	4g	cumin powder
18g	salt	4g	red chilli powder
16g	fresh coriander	1g	turmeric
8g	green chillies		

Cooked Weight 1265g

Lower Fat

620g	illish fish	36g	salt
198g	onions	14g	curry powder
40g	mix vegetable oil	6g	chillies
40g	dry mango	2g	turmeric
36g	fresh coriander		

Cooked Weight 1670g

Coat fish with turmeric and salt. Fry and set aside. Fry onions and spices in the same oil until the onions are brown. Add fish and water and garnish with coriander.

Nutrient content per 100g cooked weight

	Water	Protein	Fat	CHO	NSP	Energy	Energy
	g	g	g	g	g	kcals	kj
Average	58	14.0	20.4	1.5	0.4	245	1005
Lower fat	75	8.4	9.8	1.5	0.5	130	530

150. BENGALI KETCHKI FISH

Average

400g	ketchki fish	8g	chilli powder
162g	onions	6g	salt
32g	vegetable oil	6g	garlic
32g	curry powder	2g	turmeric
16g	fresh coriander		

Cooked Weight 515g

Lower Fat

362g	ketchki fish	10g	fresh coriander
98g	onions	10g	salt
24g	corn oil	6g	chilli powder
12g	green chillies	4g	turmeric

Cooked Weight 660g

Fry onions and garlic. Add water and spices. Then add fish and bring to the boil. Simmer and garnish with coriander.

Nutrient content per 100g cooked weight

	Water	Protein	Fat	CHO	NSP	Energy	Energy
	g	g	g	g	g	kcals	kj
Average	68	11.1	8.7	4.9	1.9	135	560
Lower fat	82	7.4	4.9	1.9	0.3	75	315

Fish dishes

151. BENGALI KOI FISH

Average

446g	koi fish
196g	onions
122g	sunflower oil
14g	green chillies
12g	fresh coriander

20g	chilli powder
16g	coriander powder
12g	salt
8g	turmeric

Cooked Weight 1060g

Lower Fat

744g	koi fish
220g	onions
82g	corn oil
18g	salt
12g	garlic

8g	green chillies
4g	cumin
2g	chilli powder
2g	turmeric
1g	coriander powder

Cooked Weight 1550g

Fry onions and spices. Add fish and water and cook. Garnish with coriander.

Nutrient content per 100g cooked weight

	Water	Protein	Fat	CHO	NSP	Energy	Energy
	g	g	g	g	g	kcals	kj
Average	68	7.2	15.8	4.1	0.3	180	750
Lower fat	76	7.4	9.6	3.4	0.2	130	535

152. BENGALI MAGUR FISH

Average

684g	magur fish
134g	onions
112g	sunflower oil
30g	fresh coriander
12g	salt

20g	green chillies
16g	red chilli powder
12g	coriander powder
6g	turmeric

Cooked Weight 1370g

Lower Fat

762g	magur fish
108g	onions
62g	mixed vegetable oil
48g	fresh coriander
18g	salt

6g	chilli powder
4g	curry powder
2g	turmeric
1g	cumin

Cooked Weight 1280g

Fry onions and spices. Add fish and water and cook. Garnish with coriander.

Nutrient content per 100g cooked weight

	Water	Protein	Fat	CHO	NSP	Energy	Energy
	g	g	g	g	g	kcals	kj
Average	77	10.3	8.8	3.0	0.2	130	535
Lower fat	78	11.8	5.4	2.9	0.2	105	440

Fish dishes

153 BENGALI PABDA FISH

Average

564g	pabda fish
196g	onions
38g	sunflower oil
30g	fresh coriander
14g	salt

6g	green chillies
4g	red chillies
3g	curry powder
2g	cumin powder
1g	turmeric

Cooked Weight 1010g

Fry onions and green chillies. Add fish and other ingredients and cook. Add water and bring to boil.

Nutrient content per 100g cooked weight

	Water	Protein	Fat	CHO	NSP	Energy	Energy
	g	g	g	g	g	kcals	kj
Average	76	11.2	5.1	4.3	0.4	105	440

154. BENGALI PRAWN BHUNA

Average

320g	prawns
134g	tinned tomatoes
102g	onions
40g	vegetable oil
40g	fresh coriander

6g	curry powder
6g	chilli powder
4g	salt
1g	turmeric

Cooked Weight 480g

Lower Fat

232g	prawns
134g	onions
60g	tomatoes
30g	sunflower oil
30g	fresh coriander

16g	salt
6g	chillies
5g	coriander
4g	turmeric
2g	red chillies

Cooked Weight 330g

Fry onions, add spices and tomatoes. Add the prawns and cook. Garnish with coriander.

Nutrient content per 100g cooked weight

	Water	Protein	Fat	CHO	NSP	Energy	Energy
	g	g	g	g	g	kcals	kj
Average	64	15.9	11.1	3.8	1.1	180	745
Lower fat	62	13.8	6.6	4.8	0.8	135	555

155. BENGALI RUI (ROHU) FISH

Average

236g	rui fish	6g	chilli powder
94g	onions	4g	coriander powder
40g	corn oil	4g	salt
3g	turmeric	1g	bay leaf

Cooked Weight 465g

Rub salt and turmeric into fish and fry. Separately fry onions with other spices. Add fried fish, water and cook.

Lower Fat

900g	rui fish	6g	chilli powder
190g	onions	6g	green chillies
92g	corn oil	4g	coriander powder
16g	salt	2g	cumin
10g	garlic	2g	turmeric

Cooked Weight 1570g

Fry onions and spices. Add fish and water and cook.

Nutrient content per 100g cooked weight

	Water	Protein	Fat	CHO	NSP	Energy	Energy
	g	g	g	g	g	kcals	kj
Average	74	9	9.8	1.7	0.3	125	525
Lower fat	77	9.8	6.8	1.1	0.2	105	430

156. BENGALI RUI (ROHU) FISH AND POTATO

Average

446g	rui fish	6g	chilli powder
296g	potatoes	3g	fresh coriander
98g	onions	2g	coriander powder
66g	corn oil	2g	garlic
8g	salt	1g	turmeric

Cooked Weight 1044g

Fry fish and remove. Fry onions and spices. Add water and potatoes. Then add fish and cook.

Nutrient content per 100g cooked weight

	Water	Protein	Fat	CHO	NSP	Energy	Energy
	g	g	g	g	g	kcals	kj
Average	75	8.3	7.1	5.7	0.5	120	490

Fish dishes

157. BENGALI SARDINE FISH CURRY

Average

116g	fresh sardines	6g	chilli powder
40g	onions	1g	salt
16g	vegetable oil	1g	turmeric
8g	green chillies		

Cooked Weight 362g

Fry onion and spices. Add fish and water and cook.

Nutrient content per 100g cooked weight

	Water	Protein	Fat	CHO	NSP	Energy	Energy
		g	g	g	g	kcals	kj
Average	82	7	7.7	1.1	0.2	100	410

158. BENGALI TENGRA FISH

Average

194g	tengra fish	2g	salt
38g	onions	1g	garlic
26g	corn oil	1g	chilli powder
6g	green chillies	1g	coriander
6g	fresh coriander	1g	turmeric

Cooked Weight 330g

Lower Fat

606g	tengra fish	16g	salt
224g	onions	8g	curry powder
56g	corn oil	8g	chilli powder
10g	fresh garlic	1g	bay leaf
10g	fresh coriander	1g	turmeric

Cooked weight 1040g

Fry onions and spices. Add fish, water and cook.

Nutrient content per 100g cooked weight

	Water	Protein	Fat	CHO	NSP	Energy	Energy
	g	g	g	g	g	kcals	kj
Average	71	11.7	11.9	2.5	0.2	165	690
Lower fat	71	11.8	9.3	3.7	0.3	145	600

Sweet Dishes

Sweet dishes

159. PUNJABI DHURI (OAT PORRIDGE)

Average

600g milk	40g ghee
275g porridge oats	20g almonds
80g sugar	

Cooked Weight 2240g

Lower Fat

1200g water	60g sugar
550g milk	12g ghee
300g porridge	

Cooked Weight 2010g

Cook all ingredients except almonds together till the porridge thickens. Add almonds (if used).

Nutrient content per 100g cooked weight

	Water	Protein	Fat	CHO	NSP	Energy	Energy
	g	g	g	g	g	kcals	kj
Average	79	2.6	4.4	14.0	0.9	100	430
Lower fat	79	2.7	3.0	15.3	1.0	95	400

160. PAKISTANI KHEER (RICE PUDDING)

Average

1560g full fat milk	
398g sugar	
126g rice	
(water)	

Cooked Weight 2020g

Cook rice in water. Boil milk and add drained rice. Add sugar and cook till done.

Lower Fat

80g rice	6g ground coconut
28g sugar	4g almonds
25g milk	4g pistachios

Cooked Weight 820g

Boil milk and add rice. Cook stirring constantly. Add sugar and nuts. Cook till done.

Nutrient content per 100g cooked weight

	Water	Protein	Fat	CHO	NSP	Energy	Energy
		g	g	g	g	kcals	kj
Average	65	2.9	3.0	29.4	Tr	150	635
Lower fat	89	1.1	1.2	11.7	0.2	60	255

Sweet dishes

161. PAKISTANI SEVIA (SWEET VERMICELLI)

Average

454g	milk	25g	almonds
134g	sugar	20g	dry coconut
76g	vermicelli	5g	cardamom
36g	vegetable ghee		

Cooked Weight 750g

Heat ghee. Add cardamom, vermicelli, coconut, and sugar. Then add milk and cook till done. Sprinkle with nuts before serving.

Nutrient content per 100g cooked weight

	Water	Protein	Fat	CHO	NSP	Energy	Energy
	g	g	g	g	g	kcals	kj
Average	55	3.7	10.8	30	0.9	225	945

162. PAKISTANI ZARDA (SWEET RICE)

Average

576g	basmati rice	24g	almonds
134g	sugar	2g	cardamom
90g	sunflower oil		

Cooked Weight 1075g

Soak rice for a short while. Add boiled water and drain when half cooked. Separately add oil, sugar, cardamom, and nuts and fry. Add water and rice and bring to a boil. Let simmer till done.

Lower Fat

260g	basmati rice	40g	sultanas
190g	sugar	34g	dry coconut
50g	almonds	1g	cardamom
48g	vegetable ghee		

Cooked Weight 1270g

Boil rice and drain. Fry cardamom in ghee till brown. Add sugar and water and bring to a boil. Add rice, nuts, and dry fruit. Bring to a boil. Simmer till done.

Nutrient content per 100g cooked weight

	Water	Protein	Fat	CHO	NSP	Energy	Energy
	g	g	g	g	g	kcals	kj
Average	29	4.5	9.9	56.0	0.4	330	1380
Lower fat	54	2.6	7.8	34.7	0.7	216	900

163. ISMAILI THEPLA

Average

296g   white flour
168g   sunflower oil - used in frying
126g   white sugar
56g   egg (1)
68g   semi-skimmed milk
2g   cardamom
2g   nutmeg

Cooked Weight 638g

Add egg, sugar and spices to the flour and bind with warm milk. Stand for a while. Roll out and cut into circles or triangles. Fry in oil till brown.

Nutrient content per 100g cooked weight

	Water	Protein	Fat	CHO	NSP	Energy	Energy
	g	g	g	g	g	kcals	kj
Average	11.6	5.9	26.6	57.4	1.4	475	1995

164. BENGALI SHANDESH (SWEET)

Average

80g   plain white flour
30g   corn oil used in frying
14g   white sugar
       Water

Cooked Weight 190g

Lower Fat

318g   white sugar   226g   plain white flour
162g   rice flour   88g   sunflower oil used in frying

Cooked Weight 1110g

Mix sugar and flours with water to runny mixture and whisk (like pancake mix consistency). Heat oil. Spoon mixture into hot oil and fry.

Nutrient content per 100g cooked weight

	Water	Protein	Fat	CHO	NSP	Energy	Energy
	g	g	g	g	g	kcals	kj
Average	41	3.9	16.2	40.0	1.3	310	1300
Lower fat	47	2.9	8.3	57.6	0.9	305	1290

APPENDIX 1

a. **Commonly consumed traditional foods and dishes, listed in decreasing order of use, for the five South Asian Groups described**

1. **Punjabi Sikhs**
   Chapati/Roti
   Mixed Indian tea
   Yogurt
   Chicken curry
   Paratha
   Rice
   Masoor dhal
   Chana dhal
   Mixed vegetable curry
   Aubergine and potato curry
   Lamb curry
   Urad dhal
   Lamb keema (mince) curry

2. **Gujarati Hindus**
   Chapati
   Rice
   Tuwar dhal
   Kitchadi
   Potato curry
   Khadi (yogurt curry)
   Yogurt (full fat, home made)
   Papadum
   Aubergine curry
   Bhajia
   Mixed mithai (sweetmeats)
   Mixed vegetable curry
   Bhindi (okra)
   Whole mung curry
   Mung dhal
   Sev mamra (fried snack)
   Spinach curry
   Rotlo (bread)
   Aubergine and mixed vegetable curry
   Lassi (yogurt drink)
   Ganthia (fried snack)
   Dohkra (gram flour cake)
   Chevda (fried snack)
   Mango chutney
   Channa dhal
   Mixed Indian tea

3. **Bangladeshi Muslims**
   Rice
   Ukni (meat pilau)
   Chapati
   Rice pitta
   Shandesh (fried sweet)
   Masoor dhal
   Chicken curry
   Chicken and potato curry
   Chicken bhuna (dry curry)
   Chicken and vegetable curry
   Lamb chops curry
   Lamb and potato curry
   Lamb keema (mince) curry
   Lamb and vegetable curry
   Bual fish curry
   Illish fish curry
   Rui fish curry
   Gargot fish curry
   Koi fish curry
   Prawn bhuna (dry curry)
   Prawn and vegetable curries
   Tengra fish curry
   Ketchki fish curry
   Pabda fish curry
   Magur fish curry
   Baing (baim) fish and potato curry
   Shutki (dried) gojar fish curry
   Shutki (dried) hidol fish curry
   Egg curry
   Potato bhaji *
   Mixed vegetable bhaji
   Spinach bhaji
   Cauliflour bhaji
   Bhindi (okra) bhaji
   Aubergine bhaji
   Samosas
   Paratha
   Rui fish and potato curry
   Sardine curry.

   * bhaji is used to describe a variety of stir fried vegetable dishes.

4. Pakistani Muslims

Roti
Rice
Meat pilau
Vegetable pilau
Stuffed paratha
Chicken curry
Lamb curry
Aloo ghosht (lamb and potato)
Ghosht palak (lamb and spinach)
Keema (mince lamb) curry
Aloo keema (lamb and mince) curry
Kebab
Kofta (meatballs) curry
Roast chicken
Whole chickpeas (channa) curry
Channa dhal
Masoor dhal
Mung dhal
Mixed vegetable curry
Potato curry
Bhindi (okra)
Palak (spinach)
Pakora (bhajia)
Samosas
Kheer (rice pudding)
Sevia (sweet vermicelli)
Mithai (sweetmeats)
Biryani (meat and rice)
Daal maash
Matar keema (lamb and peas)
Paratha
Khadi (yogurt curry)

5. Ismaili Muslims

Rice
Rotli
Kitchadi (rice and lentils)
Ukni (meat pilau)
Biryani (meat and rice)
Chicken curry
Meat curry
Keema curry (mince)
Masala fish and potatoes
Mixed vegetable curry
Whole mung curry
Dhal (daar)
Dhokra
Thepla (fried sweet biscuit)
Kebab
Samosas
Bhajias
Paratha
Ganthia (fried snack)
Chicken Pilau
Khadi (yogurt curry)

b. Fish consumed by the Bangladeshi Group in Britain

Sylheti name	Taxonomic name	Type of fish
Ayr / Gargot	Mystus seenghala	White
Boal	Wallago attu	White
Chital	Notopterus chitala	White
Rui / Rohu / Ruee	Labeo rohita	White
Kanla	-	White
Ketchki	-	White
Shoal	-	White
Gojar	-	White
Magur	Clarius batrachus	White
Pabda	Challichorus pabo	White
Baim / Baing	Mastocembellus armatus	Oily
Hidol	-	Oily
Sardines	Sardina pilchardis	Oily
Tengra	Mystus vittatus	Oily
Illish / Hilsa	Clupea ilisha	Oily
Koi	Anabus testudineus	Oily
Pangas	Pangasius	Oily

APPENDIX 2

Calculations used to estimate vitamin losses in cooked foods

Nutrient losses were determined as described in The Composition of Foods (Southgate and Paul, 1991) using the factors shown below. For composite dishes the factors are applied according to the main ingredient in the recipe - different factors were not assigned to each individual ingredient. Thus these can only be regarded as estimates.

Vegetable dishes

Carotene	0%
Vitamin E	0%
Thiamin	20%
Riboflavin	20%
Niacin	20%
Vitamin B6	20%
Folate	50%
Vitamin C	50%

	Fish and Fish dishes		Meat and meat - based dishes	
	Boiled/ poached	Fried/ grilled	Roast/grilled fried	Meat dishes
Vitamin A	-	-	0	0
Vitamin E	0	0	20	20
Thiamin	10	20	20	20
Riboflavin	0	20	20	20
Niacin	0	20	20	20
Vitamin B6	10	20	20	20
Vitamin B12	0	0	20	20
Folate	0	0	-	50

Cereal dishes

	Boiling	Baking
Thiamin	40	25
Riboflavin	40	15
Niacin	40	5
Vitamin B6	40	25
Folate	50	50

Rice dishes such as biryani containing meat were considered as meat dishes.

APPENDIX 3

Missing values in foods which have been substituted with those from similar foods or indicated as missing values

Beans and pulses

Black gram / urad	NSP, B6, folate, Vitamin E, Cl
Chick peas (channa), split	NSP,
Red lentils (masoor)	Vitamin E
Mung beans	NSP, B6, Vitamin E
Pigeon peas (tuwar)	NSP, B6, Vitamin E

Vegetables

Courgettes	Vitamin E
Gourd - bottle	Sugar, starch, NSP, fatty acids, B6, vitamin E
Gourd - karela	Fatty acids, B6, vitamin E
Gourd - ridge	NSP, B6, vitamin E
Gourd - snake	Sugar starch, NSP, fatty acids, B6, vitamin E
Gourd - tinda	NSP, fatty acids, Zn, B6, folate, vitamin E
Marrow	NSP, B6,
Mixed vegetables (frozen)	NSP, fatty acids, vitamin E
Mooli (white radish)	NSP, Cl, Cu.
Peppers capsicum - chilli	NSP, fatty acids, Cu, B6, vitamin E
Peas, dried split	Folate
Coconut - creamed	NSP, B6, folate.

Cereals

Basmati rice	NSP, fatty acids, Na, K, Mg, Cl, Zn, Cu, thiamin, riboflavin, B6, folate, vitamin E
Chapati flour, brown	NSP
Chapati flour, white	NSP
Semolina	Fatty acids
Vermicelli	NSP, sugar, starch, Zn, B6, folate
Rice flour	NSP, fatty acids, sugar, Zn, folate, vitamin E

In addition to the above it is noted that many of the pulses and some vegetables contain significant amounts of oligosaccharides which are not accounted for in the food data base (Holland et al. 1991). Thus when recipes contain significant amounts of the following ingredients the values for starch and sugars will not add up to the value for total available carbohydrate : -

black gram (urad), broad beans, chick peas, haricot beans, lentils, mung beans, pigeon peas (tuwar), red kidney beans, soya beans, peas, cabbage, carrots, leeks, onions, capsicums, squash and sweetcorn.

COMMON AND TAXONOMIC NAMES OF INGREDIENTS USED

Food name	Alternative name	Taxonomic name
Almonds		Prunus dulcis (varieties)
Aubergine	eggplant, brinjal	Solanum melongena
Beef		Bos taurus
Bottle gourd		Legenaria sicereria
Cabbage	gobi, kobi	Brassica olereacea
Cardamom	ellaichi	Elletaria cardamomum
Carrots	gajjar	Daucus carota
Cauliflower	phool gobi	Brassica olereacea var botrytis
Chick peas	channa, yellow gram	Cicer arietinum
Chicken		Gallus domestica
Chilli green	pimento, peppers, hari murch	Capsicum annuum
Chilli red	sabut lal murch	Capsicum annuum
Cloves	long, laung	Eugenia aromatica
Coconut	nariyal	Cocus nucifera
Coriander seed	dhania, dhania pattar, dhania sabz	Coriandrum sativum
Coriander leaves	hara dhania	Coriandrum sativum
Courgette	zucchini	Cucerbita pepo
Cumin	zeera, jeera, cummin,pisa	Cuminum cyminum
Fenugreek	methi	Trogonella foenum-graecum
French beans	green beans	Phaseolus vulgaris
Garlic	lassan, lehsan	Allium sativum
Ginger	adrak	Zingiber officinale
Ginger ground	sonth	Zingiber officinale
Green pepper	capsicum, sweet peppers	Capsicum annuum var grossum
Guwar	guar, cluster beens	Cyanopsis tetragonoloba
Hing	asafoetida	Ferula asafoetida
Karela	bitter gourd	Momordica charantia
Lamb		Ovis aries
Lemons		Citrus limon
Lentils , green and brown	continental lentils,masur	Lens esculenta
Lentils , red	masoor dhal, masur dhal	Lens esculenta
Marrow		Cucerbita pepo
Mooli	white radish	Raphanus sativa
Moth - bean	mat - bean	Phaseolus aconitifolius
Mung beans	green gram, golden gram,moong	Phaseolus aures
Mustard black	rai, kimcea,sarson	Brassica nigra
Nutmeg	jaiphal	Myristica fragrans

Food name	Alternative name	Taxonomic name
Oats		Avena sativa
Okra	bhindi,bhinda,bhendi, lady's fingers	Hibiscus esculentus
Onions	dungli,kanda,piyaz	Allium ciea
Peas	mattar ,vatana	Pisum sativum
Pepper black	kali mirich	Piper nigrum
Pigeon pea	toor, tuwar, dar	Cajanus cajan
Potatoes	aloo	Solanum tuberosum
Prawns		Puleamon serratus
Rice		Oryza sativa
Ridge gourd		
Runner beans		Phaseolus coccineus
Saithe	coley	Pollachius virens
Sardines		Sardina pilchardus
Semolina	soojee	Ttriticum aestivum
Soya beans		Glycine max
Spinach	palak, saag	Spinachia oleracea
Tindora	tinda	
Tomatoes		Lycopersicum esculentum
Turmeric	haldi	Curcuma longa
Urad gram	black gram, urad	Vigna mungo
Wheat		Ttriticum aestivum

REFERENCES

Association of Official Analytical Chemists. (1975). Official methods of analysis. 12the edition, Washington DC: William Horwitz.

Englyst, H.N. and Cummings, J.H. (1984)
Simplified method for the measurement of total non-starch-polysaccharides by gas-liquid chromatography of constituent sugars as alditol acetates. Analyst 109, 937 - 942

Englyst, H.N. and Cummings, J.H. (1988)
An improved method for the measurement of dietary fibre as the non-starch polysaccharides in foods. J.Assoc.Off.Anal.Chem. 71, 808 - 814

Holland, B., Unwin, I..D. & Buss, D.H.. (1988). Cereals and cereal products, Supplement to McCance and Widdowson's The Composition of Foods. Cambridge: RSC

Holland, B., Welch, A.A, Unwin ID, Buss, D.H., Southgate, D.A.T. and Paul, A.A (1991) McCance and Widdowson's The Composition of Foods. (Fifth Edition). Cambridge: RSC

Holland, B., Unwin, I.D. & Buss, D.H. (1991a). Vegetables, Herbs and Spices, Supplement to McCance and Widdowson's The Composition of Foods. Cambridge: RSC.

IUPAC (1976) Standard methods for the analysis of oils, fats and soaps. 4the supplement to the 5the edition. Method II D 19. Preparation of fatty acid methyl esters. Method I D19. Gas liquid chromatography of fatty acid methyl esters.

Kassam-Khamis T.(1996) South Asian Foodways in Britain. Diversity and change and the implications for health promotion. PhD Thesis, University of London

Kassam Khamis T., Judd, P.A., Thomas, J.E., Sevak L., Reddy S., Ganatra S. (1995). Frequency of consumption and nutrient composition of composite dishes commonly consumed by South Asians originating from Gujarat and the Punjab. Journal of Human Nutrition and Dietetics 8: 265-277.

Phillips, D.R. and Wright, A. J. A. (1983) Studies on the response of *Lactobacillus casei* to folate vitamin in foods. Br J Nutr. 49, 181 - 186

Reddy, S. (1991) A comparison of the diet and health of pre-menopausal Indian and Caucasian vegetarian women. PhD Thesis , University of London

Sevak, L., McKeigue, P. M. and Marmot, M.G . (1994).
Relationship of hyperinsulinaemia to dietary intake in South Asian and European men. Am J Clin Nutr. 59, 1069 - 1074.

Tan, S.P., Wenlock, R.W. & Buss, D.H. (1985). Immigrant Foods, 2nd supplement to McCance and Widdowson's "The Composition of Foods". London: HMSO.

INDEX

Food	South Asian group	No	Page
chicken/potato curry	Bengali	137	50
chicken/potato curry	Ismaili	136	50
chickpea curry	Pakistani	68	28
chickpeas	Punjabi	64	28
courgette	Punjabi	28	20
dhal maash	Pakistani	80	32
dhal/dar	Ismaili	84	32
dhokra	Ismaili	112	40
dhudi	Gujarati	44	24
egg curry	Bengali	142	50
ganthia	Ismaili	173	64
gargot (ayr) curry	Bengali	146	56
Gojar	Gojar	183	66
gojar shutki curry	Bengali	147	56
gosht palak	Pakistani	130	46
gourd	Punjabi	42	24
gourd/potato	Punjabi	43	24
green chill/carrot	Punjabi	33	20
guar	Gujarati	50	24
hidol fish chutney	Bengali	148	56
Hidol shutki - dry	Bengali	184	66
illish fish curry	Bengali	149	56
kahdi	Gujarati	87	36
Kanla - fresh	Bengali	177	66
karela	Gujarati	49	24
karela	Punjabi	48	24
karhi	Punjabi	86	36
kebab	Bengali	170	64
kebab	Ismaili	171	64
ketchki - fresh	Bengali	178	66
ketchki fish curry	Bengali	150	56
khadi	Ismaili	88	36
khadi	Pakistani	89	36
kheer	Pakistani	160	62
kitchadi	Gujarati	91	36
kitchadi	Ismaili	92	36
kitchadi	Punjabi	90	36
kofta	Pakistani	129	46
koi fish curry	Bengali	151	56
lamb chops	Punjabi	116	46
lamb curry	Bengali	119	46
lamb curry	Ismaili	117	46

Food	South Asian group	No	Page
lamb curry	Pakistani	118	46
lamb keema	Bengali	126	46
lamb keema	Ismaili	122	46
lamb keema	Pakistani	123	46
lamb keema	Punjabi	120	46
lamb/potato curry	Punjabi	114	46
magur fish curry	Bengali	152	56
marrow	Punjabi	29	20
masala fish	Ismaili	143	56
masoor dhal	Bengali	60	28
masoor dhal	Pakistani	59	28
masoor dhal	Punjabi	55	28
masoor dhal - thick	Punjabi	56	28
masoor/mung dhal	Punjabi	57	28
masoor/mung/channa dhal	Punjabi	58	28
masoor/tomato dhal	Punjabi	54	28
matar keema	Pakistani	124	46
matar keema	Punjabi	121	46
matar paneer	Punjabi	139	50
matar paneer/potato	Punjabi	140	50
methi bhaji	Gujarati	10	16
methi paratha	Punjabi	107	40
mithai	Pakistani	176	64
mooli bhaji (miser)	Gujarati	51	24
moth dhal	Punjabi	79	32
mung curry whole	Gujarati	73	32
mung curry whole	Ismaili	75	32
mung curry whole	Punjabi	71	32
mung dhal	Pakistani	74	32
mung dhal	Punjabi	69	32
mung dhal whole	Punjabi	70	32
mung/masoor dhal	Punjabi	72	32
mung/moth dhal	Punjabi	78	32
mutton curry	Punjabi	115	46
oat porridge (dhuri)	Punjabi	159	62
pabda fish curry	Bengali	153	56
palak paneer	Punjabi	141	50
paratha	Bengali	108	40
paratha	Ismaili	174	64
paratha	Pakistani	106	40
paratha	Punjabi	105	40
peas/potato	Gujarati	53	28

Food	South Asian group	No	Page
spinach/potato	Punjabi	11	16
tengra fish curry	Bengali	158	56
thepla	Ismaili	163	62
tindora	Gujarati	46	24
tindora	Punjabi	45	24
toor dhal	Punjabi	81	32
turia/potato	Gujarati	47	24
tuwar dhal	Gujarati	82	32
urad dhal	Punjabi	76	32
urad/tomato dhal	Punjabi	77	32
mixed veg. bhaji	Bengali	5	16
mixed veg.curry	Gujarati	2	16
mixed veg.curry	Ismaili	3	16
mixed veg.curry	Pakistani	4	16
mixed veg.curry	Punjabi	1	16
zarda	Pakistani	162	62